A European Life

from war to peace

Memoirs
by
Michael Tracy

HERMITAGE

ISBN 978-2-930590-00-4

Other books by Michael Tracy:

Government and Agriculture in Western Europe, 1880–1988 (3rd edition, 1989)

Food and Agriculture in a Market Economy – an introduction to theory, practice and policy (1993)

The World of the Edwardian Child, as seen in Arthur Mee's Children's Encyclopaedia, 1910 (2008)

To those who think Europe matters,
and even more so, to those who don't.

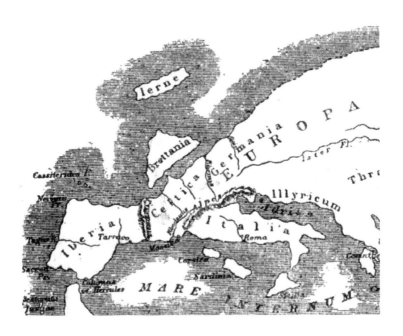

One of the earliest maps of Europe
by the Greek geographer Strabo (63/64 BC – ca. AD 24)
(from Wikimedia Commons)

The cover illustration of "Europa and the bull"
is from a Greek vase of the fourth century BC
by courtesy of the Kunsthistorisches Museum, Vienna

CONTENTS

Foreword

Michael's memoirs were an enjoyable read for my wife Katherine and myself. We traversed the same paths in the later stages of our professional lives.

Reading the memoirs underlined thoughts I often have as a university teacher about so-called "career planning". I have never thought of it as in any way useful in my own case since what I ended up doing was mostly surprising and governed by events beyond my control. I think I was right when I used to advise my students to pursue what they were good at, provided they enjoyed it. Michael did that too, moving on from his studies of languages at school to economics at Cambridge University, and moving from one post to another.

His other interests, in music, art and history clearly deepened his enjoyment of Europe and forged his European identity and maybe even pride in being a "European". I often think that belonging to a large and most diverse Europe strengthens the need to have personal roots and a sense of belonging –an idea that has eluded the euro-sceptics.

There seems to be a pattern to the events that provided Michael's opportunities. There was his childhood in the war which set the conditions for the European idea; Fettes College still educating people for the Empire and coincidentally fitting him out for Europe. Via various international experiences, he reached the heart of the European Community in the Council Secretariat, where he was in a privileged position to see all sides of EU decision-making in the Council. Then in his maturity he was able during the 1990s to offer through his own efforts a great deal to the "new market States" of Central/Eastern Europe. This is a good story and he tells it well.

Reading between the lines it seems to me that Michael enjoyed academia and the experiences in Central/Eastern Europe because of the folks he met and the responses he got. I can relate to those experiences having been myself an EU consultant in the 1990s. The excitement and privilege of helping in the accession process was however tempered by darker moments such as being checked out by internal security services, upsetting Commission officials and the day to day difficulties of understanding and working within unfamiliar systems. On more than one occasion I found myself tempted to go home and leave them to it and even got as far as the threshold of the travel agents. Two things kept me going as I know was the case for Michael: 1) the young people and especially their humour and 2) despite official terms of reference, the real one was simply to be with them in a highly uncertain and daunting new enterprise. EU membership was not a certain outcome and our presence was some kind of reminder that accession was real and we were in it with them.

I concur with Michael's hints at "carpet bagger" types of consultants. Of course we were different! Also with his hints at the insensitivity and ineffectiveness of some international missions. I think there are perhaps some unpalatable truths here for posterity. On the one hand you are working for the host government (probably at too high a level) according to a contract which in the light of experience was usually ill drafted, and on the other, since the Commission was usually paying you, they expected you to heed their edicts – two masters.

Concerning Michael's last chapter, three things come to mind. Firstly the strange association of the UK Conservative party in the European Parliament. Do the last European elections point to a retrenchment in the EU success story to the point in Britain where Europe is discounted, ignored or even discarded? The British press doesn't help and the political parties seem poorly informed about the conditions in the New Market States.

As for the chances of new Market States entering the EU, I have in the last few years spent a little time in Serbia. Seeing bright young people promenading around the streets of Belgrade reminds me of the pre-accession situation in Warsaw and Bucharest. They should join the EU if their potential contribution both to Serbia and the rest of the EU is not to be wasted as has been shown by the Polish experience. But can we cope with all these independent splinters of the former Yugoslavia? It seems crazy to accept them as fully independent units in view of the complications of an EU – 35!

Finally Turkey, immigration and what we term "fortress Europe". I am not so clear on Turkey as Michael in that I can see some common external threat such as energy supplies or a nuclear Iran tipping the balance in favour of accession. I have not met many Turks but again the young folks I have met did impress me. A strengthened neighbourhood policy and bilateral trade deals seem to offer the most hope, especially given the slowness or potential failure of the "Doha" international trade negotiations. North Africa is perhaps not emphasised enough in these memoirs: it seems to be a major source and route for immigration. Can we moderate the unseemly and degrading scenes at our borders by fostering development at source?

Dr. Graham Dalton

Aberdeen University

Preface

This is my story of Europe's path from conflict to co-operation, from war to relative peace, and of the movement towards greater unity among European countries.

I spent my childhood in the shadow of war, but my professional life has been involved, in one way or another, with this European project. My personal life too has evolved in a European context, for I have visited most countries of the continent and lived in five of them.

Basically, I have come to feel "European". This is partly because I enjoy moving around between European countries and meeting people from many different backgrounds. I have an advantage in that languages usually come quite easily to me; sometimes I make do even when I only have a smattering of the language in question, and this too can lead to interesting contacts.

Moreover, my culture is essentially European. We all have different views of what "culture" means, and I can only speak for myself. As an amateur pianist, music is important to me, and music transcends national boundaries. I think particularly of Bach, Handel, Haydn, Mozart, Schubert, Beethoven – all Germanic composers – but since I like accompanying I also enjoy the English song tradition from Purcell to Benjamin Britten. My favourite operas include Mozart's "Magic Flute" and Richard Strauss' "Rosenkavalier".

As for literature: in my school days we studied the great English authors. Chaucer, Milton, Shakespeare and the "King James" edition of the Bible remain for me the foundations of the English language. Then – specialising in Modern Languages – I studied the French and German classics in the original. Other classics, particularly the Russians, I read in translation. More recently I have discovered Spanish literature in the original (this includes twentieth-century South American writers).

I also enjoy art – painting – though I am no expert in the field. Living in Belgium, there has been plenty of opportunity to see the works of the Flemish primitives and of the Dutch school, particularly in the Groninge and Memling Museum in Bruges and the Mauritshuis in The Hague. To my mind, two of the most wonderful paintings in the world are Van Eyck's "Mystic Lamb" in Antwerp cathedral (which I first saw when it was in the original chapel for which it was painted) and Rembrandt's "Prodigal Son" in the Hermitage in St. Petersburg.

These – to quote a certain musical comedy – are "some of my favourite things". Not that European culture necessarily excludes others: I practice yoga and Tai Chi, and even qualified as a teacher of Ikebana (Japanese-style flower arrangement). And as I said, everyone can have a different view. I am well aware that that I benefited from an excellent education, and that most of the subsequent young generations will not have had that advantage. On the other hand, they can travel much more easily, and may thus acquire other European references.

In the lengthy discussions which finally produced the "Lisbon Treaty" – which I discuss in my last chapter – there was difficulty in defining European values. The French ex-President Giscard d'Estaing, who chaired those talks, wanted to put in references going back to Europe's Greco-Roman origins (he even wanted a citation from Thucydides, in Greek, at the very beginning – hardly likely to have much popular appeal). He also wanted to stress the values of the Enlightenment, while other participants insisted on mention of God and the Judeo-Christian tradition.

It seems obvious to me that, whatever one's religious stance, one cannot ignore the role of Christianity in Europe's history: it permeates our literature, art and music, and there is a church or cathedral at the heart of every village, town and city. But clearly, at the present time, mention of a particular religion can be divisive. So the Preamble to the Treaty, as finally adopted, states:

"Drawing inspiration from the cultural, religious and humanist inheritance of Europe, from which have developed the universal values of the inviolable and inalienable rights of the human person, freedom, democracy, equality and the rules of law… the Union is founded on the values of respect for human dignity, freedom, democracy, equality, the rule of law and respect for human rights, including the rights of persons belonging to minorities. These values are common to the Member States in a society in which pluralism, non-discrimination, tolerance, justice, solidarity and equality between women and men prevail." [1]

These are principles well worth stating. The European Union and its Member States have laws and institutions which should ensure their respect. The same cannot be said for all other parts of the world: not yet, regrettably, for Russia and some other countries at that end of the continent, though they share in so much of the culture of the rest of Europe.

This European stance does not mean that I give unqualified support to all that happens in "Brussels", and this book is not a tract for or against the European Union in its present form. However, its creation and prospects are the main determinants of the development of Europe as a whole, so inevitably the EU is the subject of most of my narrative. But I have also a good deal to say about my experiences in the countries of Central and Eastern Europe, including Russia, since their Communist regimes began to collapse in 1989. In the years to come, developments in Russia and in its relations with the EU may be more significant than anything that happens at the western end of the continent.

So this book is an account of my own experiences in the European context; it is not a history. A work of history requires that all relevant aspects be considered and calls for extensive sources and references; there are plenty such books on twentieth-century Europe.

I have tried to concentrate on the themes indicated by the chapter titles and their initial paragraphs and to recount only my own experience (the last chapter is an exception). Sometimes I felt that more background is required, and I have usually put this in end-notes; likewise comments arising from later knowledge, and important references. Some of these notes have become quite extensive, but they are optional reading.

This is not an autobiography: my personal life comes into the narrative only as far as this is relevant to my theme. However, since my European stance will probably sound provocative to the numerous British "euro-sceptics", a disclaimer seems necessary. I know many people – particularly but not only among those living in the Brussels area – who would also regard themselves as "Europeans": none of these would regard this stance as conflicting with their regional or national origins.

In my own case, my father was Irish and my mother Scottish; I was brought up in Scotland. Those Irish and Scottish roots have not disappeared. My father came from a farming family (Southern Irish, but Protestant) and he was a veterinary surgeon: his countryman's ways and his ease with animals have continued to influence me.[2] So has my mother's typically Scottish "hard-work ethic". I remember with affection many Scottish traditions and maintain some of them; in several places on the Continent I have found myself involved in Scottish country-dancing societies. Robert Burns has always been my favourite poet, one who speaks directly to me. My occasional visits back to Scotland have always had a special attraction for me.

The President of the European Council, Herman Van Rompuy, speaking just after his nomination on 19 November 2009, said: "if our unity is our strength, our diversity remains our wealth." I heartily agree.

Many people have helped me in preparing this book, including several who are mentioned in it, so this is an opportunity for me to recognise several friends who also, in one way or another, are leading "European" lives.

Marianne Rudnicki is the widow of the Polish writer Josef Rudnicki, whose works reflect the traumas of life under Nazi occupation and the post-war Communist regime; she is currently editing his diaries. She also runs a writing workshop in Paris, which is perhaps why she encouraged me to embark on these memoirs.

I knew Graham Dalton of Aberdeen University when he was active in Romania and Poland in the 1990s. I admired his work, especially for his humanistic approach, at a time when it was being disparaged by more technocratic colleagues. I have also visited his farm near Aberdeen. I am grateful to him and his wife Katherine for valuable comments and for contributing a Foreword – probably too generous to myself.

I first met Agata Zdanowicz at a conference in Poland in the early 1990s, when she was part of the advisory team set up by Graham Dalton in the Ministry of Agriculture. We kept in touch in subsequent years while she occupied several interesting posts relating to rural development and environment; she is now in charge of a unit in the European Commission.

Dr. Susan Senior-Nello was one of my students at the College of Europe in Bruges, and then moved on to the European University Institute in Florence. She has made valuable comments on my texts concerning these two institutions. She herself is currently preparing the third edition of her highly-regarded book on the European Union.

Professor Michel Petit is one of those French agricultural economists who has always been open to the world outside. He was President of the European Association of Agricultural Economists when in 1981 this Association held its conference in Belgrade and I (at his request) was Programme Secretary; he succeeded me at the College of Europe in Bruges; and he was Director for Agriculture in the World Bank in Washington at the time of the World Bank mission to the USSR on which I comment in Chapter VII. On these and other matters in my chapter "Academia", he has commented very helpfully (while disclaiming responsibility for the USSR mission).

Kevin Leydon, a former senior official in the Irish public sector and then in the European Commission, participated from 2002 in the work leading to the proposed European Constitution. He spent a whole afternoon guiding me through the intricacies of those discussions, which helped me greatly to understand the background to the Lisbon Treaty.

I have written in chapter V about Inessa Frantseva, who played such a valuable role helping me in two missions to Moscow in late 1991. Since then we have met or communicated from time to time, and this has helped to keep me in touch with developments in Russia. She has also commented helpfully on the relevant parts of these Memoirs, but she is not responsible for my criticisms of the current regime in my last chapter.

Christine Dickert was once my very efficient secretary in Brussels. She is German; I recruited her because I needed someone to work in both French and English, and she did this better than any of the French or English candidates! She has since moved on to much more interesting things (including yoga and aikido). As always with my drafts, she has kindly read everything with an eagle eye and suggested many improvements both in substance and in detail. Any faults that remain must arise from changes I have made subsequently.

Finally, my wife Rosalind: she was part of the British team negotiating the UK's 1973 entry to the EEC. Then – sitting behind the UK label while I was at the Council Secretariat desk – she was a fellow-sufferer in many interminable Brussels meetings on agriculture and fisheries. She now pursues her real interests as an art historian. She has contributed greatly to this work by filling in gaps in my memories and through our ongoing discussions of many relevant topics.

---

[1] Giscard d'Estaing did have a valid point about the Greco-Roman origins. As a reminder, I have chosen for the cover of this book a representation of "Europa and the bull" from a fourth-century BC vase painting by an artist working in a Greek colony in Apulia in south-east Italy; I have also reproduced on a front page a very early map of Europe by the Greek philosopher Strabo. The legend of the Phoenician princess Europa being carried off to Crete by Zeus in the form of a bull was mentioned in Homer's *Iliad* (early eighth century BC), and in subsequent centuries her name came to be attached to the continent by Greek geographers: how and why are not quite clear, but the map demonstrates that the term was definitely in use at least by the time of Strabo.

[2] The family name "Tracy" is generally associated with Ireland, yet it also appears in France: there is a village of that name in Normandy, near the landing beaches of 1945, and there is a Château de Tracy on the Loire (which produces excellent *Pouilly Fumé* wine). Knights called "Tracy" were part of the Norman invasion in 1066. Regrettably, a Sir William de Tracy was one of the four knights who murdered Thomas Becket in 1170 in Canterbury cathedral (a plaque marks the spot and names the murderers).

In due course, nobles of this name were granted lands in Ireland. While some remained as landed gentry, others eventually mingled with the native population: my father's family, having a medium-sized farm near Naas in Co. Kildare, were in this category. According to my father, the name spelt as we do signifies a Protestant family; the more usual "Tracey" spelling denotes Catholics. The use as a first name is a recent development.

An advantage for me has been that the name can be pronounced in either the English or the French way (the "a" can be like "ay" or "ah").

I. WARTIME
Scotland

On 1 September 1939 Germany – having already annexed Austria and occupied Czechoslovakia – attacked Poland. France and Britain declared war. Germany occupied Denmark in April 1940, then moved on Norway. On 9 May German forces invaded Luxembourg, then the Netherlands and Belgium. By 26 May British forces in France were encircled at Dunkirk: their evacuation lasted till 4 June. France capitulated on 22 June.

Germany and Russia having signed a non-aggression pact, Britain's only active ally was then Greece, soon to be occupied by Italy and Germany. In Western Europe, Britain stood alone.

When war broke out I was six years old, and my earliest memories are associated with those events. Though I do not remember much of the early stages – it can be difficult to distinguish some real memories from what one has subsequently learned – as the war progressed many events were clearly imprinted on my mind.

We were living in Helensburgh – a pleasant residential Scottish town on the Clyde estuary – so to some extent the war seemed far enough away. I do however remember, when the British army was cornered at Dunkirk, the broadcast appeal for boats – boats of any kind, anything that could reach the Dover straits soon enough – to go and help in the evacuation. As we know, hundreds of small boats did just that, and together with the Royal Navy and the merchant navy succeeded in getting most of the trapped soldiers across the Channel.

A German invasion was then feared. Once the evacuation from Dunkirk was completed, Winston Churchill – who had replaced Joseph Chamberlain as British Prime Minister on 13 May 1940 – gave the second of his great wartime speeches (the first – on "Blood, toil, tears and sweat" – had been to Parliament on his appointment). I can still recall that extraordinary voice, gruff yet eloquent, and the famous words: "We shall fight on the beaches, we shall fight on the landing grounds, we shall fight in the fields and in the streets, we shall fight in the hills; we shall never surrender".[1] That was the reassurance that we needed, and which Churchill continued to provide in the difficult times to follow. In this,

BBC broadcasts on the radio (we usually called it "wireless") had a vital role to play.

France capitulated soon afterwards. By this time I was sufficiently aware of the significance of these events to feel outraged: I marched up to my parents and demanded to know what small boys could do to help win the war. I was not being particularly gallant: this just reflected the determination which we all felt. I don't think that we ever really doubted that Britain would in the end defeat Nazi Germany. My parents told me that Britain had never lost a war, which was reassuring though not strictly true (it disregarded the American War of Independence, while the Crimean and the Boer Wars had not been great successes). They were not greatly surprised by the defeat of France. My father had been a volunteer in the First World War, serving in the Royal Army Veterinary Corps, and was severely wounded near the end of the war. Like many soldiers who had experienced that war, he rarely talked about it, but he did not rate French soldiers very highly: fine, he said, when they were doing well, but unreliable in defeat. (This was a soldier's point of view and probably unfair – French troops were atrociously commanded in both wars and in 1939-40 had not been given the air support they would have needed to withstand the combined attacks of Panzers and Stukas.)

My father still had his captain's uniform and I liked to get it out and try it on, and admire the medals he had got for various campaigns. It was customary then even for retired officers to be addressed according to their former rank, so he was generally called "Captain Tracy", though in fact he was a most unmilitary man. Once, for his birthday, I offered him a book on the "Great War" called *Blasting and Bombardiering*: he just said he had seen enough blasting, and I don't think he ever opened that book. My best friend was the son of a local butcher, who had been gassed in that war and his lungs had never fully recovered.

So echoes of the previous war still surrounded us. But at my age, I was unaware of the horrors of war: it seemed almost like a game. We were issued with gas masks, which we found amusing; fortunately, they never had to be used. Of course, the war dominated our playground games: with the "Battle of Britain" which began in July 1940, we would be Spitfires and Hurricanes against Heinkels and Messerschmitts – the latter of course had to be shot down so this was the unpopular role. The Spitfire was a beautiful plane: I still cannot see pictures of it without emotion.

Helensburgh, as I have written, was a residential town, of no strategic significance. However, it lay just twenty miles from Glasgow – my father travelled there to work each day, where he was Chief Veterinary Officer supervising the health of the store cattle who arrived daily on boats from Ireland, to be fattened on Scottish pastures. Eventually, Glasgow came within reach of the German bombers. The reality of war was brought home to me when he took me into the city after a night-time raid, and I saw many buildings lying in ruins. The destruction was nothing like that which London suffered. Nevertheless, some families were evacuated; for a while we had a mother with several children living in part of our house.

Across the Clyde estuary lay Greenock – clearly visible from our house on the hillside in the upper part of our town. Greenock certainly was a strategic target: with the English ports in easy reach of the Luftwaffe, most transatlantic shipping was diverted to the Clyde, to be unloaded at Greenock and its neighbour Gourock. One night the sugar refineries were bombed and went up in flames. We spent some time at our windows: the broad river, reflecting the blaze, seemed blood-red, and I felt sick. Now the war was indeed coming closer.

Strict black-out rules were imposed, and enforced by air-raid wardens who patrolled the streets at night. Windows had to be covered with adhesive sheets, and woe betide any householder who allowed a chink of light to appear. Car headlights had to be covered with special masks, making night-time driving hazardous. Sirens gave occasional air-raid warnings, when we were supposed to take shelter. We had a shelter built in our garden, half-buried and said to be able to withstand anything but a direct hit; but it was cold and damp and we never used it.

Helensburgh did once receive a few bombs, but these fell along the beach: as it happened, the tide was high and the bombs fell in the water, doing no damage. But a few miles nearer Glasgow, the village of Cardross – likewise of no military interest – suffered a severe air-raid. It was thought that the German bombers had mistaken it for Dumbarton, half-way to Glasgow, which did have some industry – Cardross lay near a peninsula sticking into the Clyde which from the air might have looked like Dumbarton castle.

Shipping in the Clyde proved interesting. In particular, the two great liners – the Queen Mary and the Queen Elizabeth – were busy trans-porting troops first from Canada, later from the USA. Much of the time, one or the other lay at anchor. I had watched the Queen Elizabeth being launched in 1938 from John Brown's shipyard, which lay across the river from my father's "lairage" where the cattle arrived. Both were beautiful ships; I preferred the Queen Mary with her three funnels. Crossing the Atlantic, they did not travel in convoy like cargo vessels but relied on their speed to outrun the U-boats; I don't think that they were ever attacked.

The Clyde itself, however, had to be protected from U-boat incursion. At the entrance to the estuary, a long boom had been placed with a narrow entrance which surface vessels could negotiate but would be difficult for a submarine. So far as I know, no U-boat ever did get through.

This did however prevent the Clyde steamers from getting any further: several towns on the northern bank had been very dependent on this service but now Rothesday in particular lay beyond this limit. Going "doon the wa'er" had been a traditional pleasure trip for Glaswegians and many others living along the river; most of the steamers – all named after characters in Walter Scott's novels – had been requisitioned as mine-sweepers, but one remained, the "Jeanie Deans". She was the oldest: it was rumoured that her sides had rusted so much that they could not be painted or the brush would go through the plates. Still, she maintained an invaluable service throughout the war. One morning after crossing the estuary on her usual run, she was greeted by agitated officials who told her she had just sailed through a minefield laid by German bombers during the night (presumably she did not have any radio connection).

Spies were thought to be everywhere. The warning "Careless talk costs lives" was pasted in railway stations and other public places.

Food rationing was introduced. It has to be remembered that before the war Britain imported more than half its food supply. Every encouragement was given to raise food production. Farmers were given price guarantees and assured that after this war – unlike the experience after the First World War – support would be maintained (a promise which was to lead to a costly agricultural policy). And anyone with a garden or plot of land was urged to "Dig for Victory". We had a sizeable vegetable garden. During the long evenings of the Scottish summer my father would work late in the garden, until the midges drove him inside. We had hens to produce eggs and for a while ducks, also goats which I learned to milk and look after. In fact, our household was more than self-sufficient for most foodstuffs, and my father would often take produce into Glasgow to hand out to colleagues.

Petrol too was severely rationed. I suppose my father had an allowance which enabled him to drive to work. At weekends we could usually drive a short distance into the hills on fishing expeditions; as I grew older I could cycle over the hill to Loch Lomond. We had kept a small motor-boat there, but with petrol rationing this had to be sold, so we now had a rowing-boat. There are beautiful islands not far away where one can swim and picnic, with Gaelic names like Inch Moan and Inch Murrin. At that time, when asked what I wanted to do when I grew up, I would say: "Keep goats on an island on Loch Lomond!".

Longer travel by car was out of the question. Our summer holidays on at least two occasions consisted of taking the West Highland Railway to an isolated hostel on Loch Ossian, north of the Moor of Rannoch, where we depended on the provisions we took with us and the trout we could catch in the loch – which fortunately were plentiful. One result was that I knew very little of Scotland until much later in life. Geography lessons had taught me that the Highlands began north of a line from Helensburgh in the west to Arbroath in the east, and that was verifiable; I do not recall much else from those lessons other than that the islands off the western shores included the delightfully-named Muck, Eigg and Rum.

So there were agreeable distractions from the war. My father had done his bit, and more, in the previous one; I had no brother to be called up for military service, so we were spared from that worry – unlike many families. The nearest relation was a cousin who was captured early on – I think before Dunkirk – and who was in a Nazi prisoner-of-war camp and was reported to be having a bad time, in chains after having tried to escape.

Like others of my age, I must have followed the events on the radio, but I have more distinct memories of the newsreels in one of the local cinemas (Helensburgh had two). I don't suppose these told the whole story – morale had to be kept up – but they were dramatic enough. After the films, the National Anthem was always played, with scenes of the Royal Family and Buckingham Place on the screen; everyone stood up for this, and it was out-of-the-question to leave before the anthem was concluded. There was great affection for King George VI, Queen Elizabeth and their two young daughters, Elizabeth and Margaret, particularly because they had refused to leave London even at the height of the blitz. There was a report that to save heating they had painted in their bath a line showing six inches depth, and would not fill the bath above this level: this was the sort of detail which made a lasting impression!

By whatever means – the BBC, and I was soon old enough to read the newspapers – I did follow the course of the war. I had a large map on the wall of my bedroom, and little flags of the combatant countries which I could pin on to show where the fighting had got to. The North African campaign was particularly dramatic. First the Italian flags moved eastwards, were thrown back by British forces, then my German and Italian flags again progressed towards the vital Suez Canal until they were stopped at El Alamein; then there was the long route back westwards until they disappeared from Africa, to be followed by the trek up the Italian peninsula. By this time, American flags had made their appearance, and of course the red hammer-and-sickle flags on the eastern frontier.

All this was exciting, and remote enough not to be too disturbing. Curiously, my personal memories seem vaguer for the later stages of the war, and are not to be distinguished in my mind from what I have subsequently learnt. I cannot now recollect, for example, what we thought about the Normandy landings. Perhaps this is partly due to the fact that, of course, we knew nothing of the extensive preparations for D-Day, though we were aware of the large number of American soldiers who had arrived in the country. Maybe also because by that time we felt that victory was assured, just a matter of time. I don't remember hearing about Arnhem or the "battle of the bulge" in the Ardennes. Subsequently, there has been so much more to learn about those set-backs as well the successes of the campaign.

Germany invaded the Soviet Union in June 1941, so I suppose my swastika flags must have marched across Russia until, after Stalingrad, the red flags pushed them back all the way to Berlin. (The Russian view of the Great Patriotic War, as I discovered much later, was very different, with some justice: for them, it is dated from the German invasion in June 1941, and they see their share of the struggle as much more significant than that of the Western powers.)

We must have celebrated VE day on 8 May 1945, but strangely I do not remember this.

The Pacific war was more remote, and here too – though I am sure we followed its course on the radio, the newspapers and the cinema newsreels – I have no clear personal memories. Except for one, dramatic, event: the explosion of the first atomic bomb over Hiroshima on 6 August, which put an end to the war against Japan. I must have known something about the potential of atomic energy.[2] When this news came over the radio: I was greatly excited and exclaimed "They've done it". My father, more aware than I was of the implications, just looked gloomy…

Looking back, I realise how fortunate we were in comparison to people in London and other southern cities, even more so as compared with those in the countries occupied by the Germans; also, how little anxious we were about the progress of the war. No doubt our parents knew much more than the children did, but kept their fears to themselves.

I feel sure that one factor keeping up morale was humour. After Chaplin's "Great Dictator" (released in 1940), no-one could take Hitler seriously, which of course was a great mistake; Mussolini likewise. And cartoonists had great fun with other Nazi leaders, particularly Goering, obese, pompous and overloaded with medals. Goebbels' ranting was mocked to such extent that his propaganda efforts had no effect whatsoever. There was an English-speaking announcer on German radio (I cannot remember how we heard this) who tried to put across their view of events, in a very posh accent: he was promptly dubbed

"Lord Haw-Haw" and was listened to only for amusement. Himmler seemed nastier and gave less scope to the caricaturists.

I have to confess that I do not remember hearing much at that time about the persecution of the Jews, although of course the "Great Dictator" made this plain.

While southern England continued to suffer from air-raids, and later on the murderous attacks by V1 and V2 rockets, for us in the north hardships were minor, and we got used to them. No-one was ever really short of food, though many people had to make do with such substitutes as dried milk and dried eggs, and obviously products previously imported were a rarity. In our case, cousins in South Africa sent a Christmas parcel each year, containing mainly dried fruits and nuts: a welcome complement to our diet.

It was reckoned that nutrition in Britain actually improved in the wartime period, as rations distributed food supplies evenly among rich and poor. Much later, working in a London research institute under the direction of a former Under-Secretary in the Ministry of Food, Ted Lloyd, I learned that at the height of the U-boat campaign the authorities had to contemplate a total cessation of food imports. In that case, the contingency plan would have been to concentrate farm production on two products, potatoes and milk. It would have been a dull diet, but it was calculated that, nutritionally, the population could just about survive.

What brought home to me the extent of the restrictions was an invitation to Denmark in the summer of 1946. Foreign travel had of course been out of the question for the duration of the war. My father, apart from his World War I service, had only been abroad once, to Switzerland and northern Italy. My mother, however, had attended a finishing school in Lausanne, and later had travelled along the Rhine. She became a teacher of modern languages, and had started me on French even before I entered the local secondary school and began French lessons there.

This generous invitation came from the Danish association of veterinary surgeons and was addressed to children of vets in Britain; they must have acted quickly after their liberation from the Germans. So I was put on a train to London where I met the rest of the group; with a minder; from there to Harwich, and then on a steamer to Esbjerg. It was a hazardous journey: there were still mines floating around in the North Sea and constant watch was kept from the prow. Moreover, this was an old boat, no doubt not much maintained during the war, and halfway across one of the two engines broke down. The sea was rough, and most of us were very sea-sick. But we landed safely, and were put on trains to our various destinations; my kind host, Dr Nielsen, had been waiting a long time at the station in Odense for our delayed train.

In Odense I enjoyed visiting the house of Hans Andersen; I still have a delightful illustrated edition of his stories, in Danish. The town also, I discovered, had a cricket club. I'm afraid I must have made a nuisance of myself by telling everyone how the game should be played properly, but they were all very polite and welcoming. The family also had a little summer house on the beach where we spent much of the time.

Danish agriculture had been maintained in good condition throughout the war – the Germans needed its output to supply part of their own needs. There was still rationing, in principle, but as compared with Britain (where rationing continued for several years) food was good and plentiful. A particular delight was to visit a cheese shop – in Britain one just asked for "cheese", always some Cheddar-type – but here was a great variety; moreover, you could ask to taste a slice before buying.

The other delight was to be taken to Copenhagen by Lis, the daughter of the family (I was now twelve and she was about twenty). Copenhagen seemed then a wonderful city, and has remained so for me ever since, with its Little Mermaid, its canals, the Round Tower, the dragon-tail spire of the Exchange. Above all, for a small boy, the Tivoli: its entertainments, the fireworks every evening and its lights. Then I realised what a dull country Britain had become: everything here was bright, clean and enjoyable.

So this was my first experience of another country, and I found it very exciting. I learnt as much Danish as I could – its grammar is relatively easy – and subsequently have tried always to learn something of the language of any country I have visited: an investment in time which has always borne fruit.

Denmark had suffered much less from the war than any other combatant or occupied country. Even their Jewish population was mostly saved: the Nazi forces gave up trying to enforce the yellow star when it was reported that the royal family would be the first to wear them, and many Jews were helped across the Great Belt to Sweden. Also, there had been very little air-raid destruction.

A couple of years later, an exchange arrangement with a German boy took me to Hameln, passing through Hannover. During the latter stages of the war, I had been excited by news of "thousand-bomber raids" on Germany. Now I saw what those air-raids had done to a major German city: around the main station, every building still lay in ruins. And I was on the way to stay with a German family – who of course received me very kindly.

[1] That speech by Churchill in June 1940 must rank with Abraham Lincoln's Gettysburg address for its role in history. It is worth quoting the essential passage in full:

"Even though large tracts of Europe and many old and famous States have fallen or may fall into the grip of the Gestapo and all the odious apparatus of Nazi rule, we shall not flag or fail. We shall go on to the end, we shall fight in France, we shall fight on the seas and oceans, we shall fight with growing confidence and growing strength in the air, we shall defend our Island, whatever the cost may be, we shall fight on the beaches, we shall fight on the landing grounds, we shall fight in the fields and in the streets, we shall fight in the hills; we shall never surrender, and even if, which I do not for a moment believe, this Island or a large part of it were subjugated and starving, then our Empire beyond the seas, armed and guarded by the British Fleet, would carry on the struggle, until in God's good time, the New World, with all its power and might, steps forth to the rescue and the liberation of the old."

One can easily construct a "what-if" scenario: without Churchill, Britain might have been invaded after Dunkirk, or would have made a pact with Hitler. Hitler could then have put all his forces into conquering Russia and might well have succeeded. Mussolini would have dominated North Africa, probably including the Suez Canal. Would the USA then have stepped forth to the rescue of Europe, as Churchill hinted? More probably, it would have been fully occupied with Japan, which would have been encouraged in its own imperialist ambitions; Pearl Harbour or something like it would still have happened; probably Burma and India, maybe Australia and New Zealand, would have fallen to the Japanese. And who would have got the atom bomb first?

I am well aware that Churchill has been subject to much criticism, for his idiosyncrasies and for strategic blunders (cf. for example Peter Clarke, *The Last Thousand Days of the British Empire*, 2007, or Nigel Knight, *The Greatest Briton Unmasked*, 2008). But I am here writing of what I and many others felt at the time. It is noteworthy that Peter Clarke, after laying bare all Churchill's faults (particularly at Yalta) makes a similar observation: "Had he been otherwise, everything would have been otherwise. Had he not been Churchill, he would not have pitched the British Empire into an all-or-nothing gamble to defy Hitler in 1940, with little support from the United States and none at all from the Soviet Union, by offering the British people his simple policy: victory at all costs." (*op. cit.* p. 223)

[2] My awareness of the power of the atom may have come from Arthur Mee's *Children's Encyclopædia* which already in its first edition of 1910 (the one we

had at home) had forecast the use of atomic power for pacific purposes, but in a distant future. The relevant passage (p. 4323) reads: "The time will come – perhaps not for hundreds of years – when mankind will be able to tap this energy inside the atom, and use it as a source of heat – to drive ships and to do work of every kind".

My book *The World of the Edwardian Child* is based on that edition of Mee's work, which gives remarkable insights into life and thought at the beginning of the twentieth century, just before the cataclysm of the First World War.

II. POST-WAR
Edinburgh (public school) and Cambridge

After the war, the countries of Central/Eastern Europe which had been liberated by the Red Army remained under Soviet domination. The three Baltic States, annexed by the Soviet Union, lost any hope of regaining their short-lived pre-war independence. Churchill declared that an "Iron Curtain" had descended over Europe.

Germany was initially divided into four zones, occupied respectively by Russia, Britain, France and the United States; Berlin, within the Soviet zone, was also divided. In March 1948 the Russians blocked both road and rail access to Berlin: the Western allies responded with an airlift of food and other supplies, which lasted until the Russian blockade was lifted in May the following year. Shortly afterwards, the western powers handed over the administration of their three zones to the government of a new Federal Republic of Germany. In response the Russians set up the German Democratic Republic.

In August 1947 India and Pakistan gained their independence, marking the end of Britain's imperial powers.

These were momentous years, tragic for the populations of Central Europe and fraught with danger for the world at large, as former allies – soon armed with nuclear weapons – confronted each other.

However, I have no significant personal memories, as the pre-occupations of school life crowded out everything else. I had received an excellent primary education at the local State school – "Hermitage" – in Helensburgh, and my mother, who as a former teacher took special interest in this matter, put me up for a scholarship to Fettes College in Edinburgh. This was – and is – one of the foremost Scottish "public schools", which of course are not public at all but on the contrary used to be the preserve of a wealthy elite. In 1945, however, Fettes had appointed a new headmaster, Donald Crichton-Miller, and took a modest step towards democracy by offering six scholarships to boys from the State system, one of which I succeeded in obtaining in 1946.

This has little to do with my European theme, but the public school system has a good deal to do with how Britain trains – or used to train –

its future leaders, and is therefore worth some comment. Fettes was founded only in 1870, but it carried over the traditions of the English public school – it has often been referred to as "the Eton of Scotland". Another democratic reform by 1946 was that top hats were abolished: our daily wear consisted of corduroy jerkins with grey trousers (or a kilt), though suits were required on Sundays, and if we went into the town (permission required) we were supposed to wear a bowler hat – most embarrassing when sitting in an Edinburgh tram!

I owe a great deal to Fettes. The education was generally good, in some respects excellent. There was a mathematics teacher who only succeeded in convincing me that I was no good at maths, but probably that was my fault. Latin – still an important subject – was taught by my housemaster, H.F. Macdonald, who was of the old school and made the topic excruciatingly boring. As soon as I had obtained the School Certificate – Fettes applied the Oxford and Cambridge system – I had no hesitation in choosing Modern Languages and English for the next two years working towards the Higher Certificate, then a third year of Modern Languages alone in preparation for Oxbridge scholarships. In this I benefited enormously from an admirable teacher, R.A. Cole-Hamilton, all the more so because in the final year we were just three in the class. By this time we knew our French and German sufficiently to concentrate on literature: we read our way through the great classics, taking parts in the plays of Molière, Corneille, Racine, and of Goethe, Schiller, Hebbel and others. We ended up among the small number of scholars who have actually studied *Faust Part II*. [1]

There were also stimulating out-of-class activities. My interest in music began at Fettes, despite being discouraged by my first piano teacher. There was singing in chapel, a school orchestra, plays; we even produced operas, including Smetana's *Bartered Bride* and – incredibly, in view of the staging difficulties – Weber's *Freischütz*. There was a debating society – important preparation for political life. We could learn Highland dancing (Highland Fling, Sword Dance and the lesser-known *Seann Truibhas*) from a former Pipe-Major: this was one of my favourite activities, and I captained a team which competed with other schools.

Attendance at "chapel" every morning during the week and for a longer service on Sundays was compulsory. (There must have been some Jewish boys, but the rule applied to all.) The chapel was in the centre of the main building, in neo-Gothic style, and had stained-glass windows which I found very beautiful. There were two chaplains, Presbyterian and Episcopalian (the Scottish version of Anglican). I don't remember much about their preaching, but the hymns were enjoyable. Evening prayers were held in each "House", led by the housemaster: this was quite a comforting occasion, with beautiful hymns such as "Abide with me, fast falls the eventide" (in due course I took my turn at the piano to accompany these hymns) and the glorious language of the book of "Common Prayer". What could be more succinct and meaningful than the prayer "Lighten our darkness, we beseech thee O Lord; and by thy great mercy defend us from all perils and dangers of this night"?

It was largely through singing and playing hymns that I learnt to read music, and it gave me a good sense of harmony. When our voices broke we descended from soprano to tenor or bass. Once, all those who could sing the parts participated in a performance of Bach's *St. Matthew Passion* in the Usher Hall (Edinburgh's main concert-hall). We had worked hard to learn the chorales, which we found quite difficult. With choirs from other schools, we filled the floor of the hall and we all rose to sing when the chorales came along. That was my first and very moving musical experience.

Sport had always been a very important feature in the public school system – the Duke of Wellington is reported to have said that "the battle of Waterloo was won on the playing-fields of Eton" – and rugby was by far the most important sport, with cricket in the summer as a second-best. When there was an international rugby match at Murrayfield, the whole school was marched there to watch. Some of our masters had probably been appointed more because they had played rugby for Scotland than for their academic record, so we were well coached. Some sporting activity was obligatory every afternoon except Sunday, whatever the weather – in the winter, with a cold wind blowing off the North Sea, conditions could be dour. Alternatives were hockey, "fives" or squash. Failing all of these, the "school run" was obligatory: several times round the extensive school grounds, on a path which in winter-time was either frozen or muddy.

We played hard, but we were also expected to play fair. This was also part of the training of a "gentleman". If we won, we were not to crow over our opponent; if we lost, we were not to show disappointment. If we were hurt, the motto was "grin and bear it"; injuries were frequent at rugby (I sustained a shoulder dislocation). Once my "house" was playing a cricket match when a batsman on the opposing side was piling up the runs. Our captain put me on to bowl – I had become a fast though rather inaccurate bowler – and told me to get the batsman out however I could. So I bowled a number of "bouncers" aimed more at his head than the wicket: he panicked, made a mistake and that was the end of his innings. I felt quite pleased with myself until our housemaster, who had been watching the match, called me over and gave me a severe dressing-down: such behaviour was "not cricket". [2]

In many other ways, the system was tough. Windows beside our beds had to be left open at least six inches whatever the weather (not surprisingly, we seemed to have colds most of the time). Cold showers were obligatory in the morning, except for prefects who could bask in warm water while watching to make sure that everyone else had their cold douche. (The cold shower has become a lifetime habit, though now I start with a hot one.)

One afternoon a week was given over to military training – the "corps", which was commanded by one of the masters, also an army major. We had army uniforms; besides basic drill, we learnt to handle a rifle and – more usefully – to read maps. In our last year we had a compulsory week at an army camp where we graduated to machine-guns and mortars, with live ammunition. We could be promoted up to the rank of sergeant (I only got as far as Lance-Corporal). With the certificate we obtained, we were assured of an immediate officer's commission if and when we entered military service (which at the time was still compulsory in principle but was being phased out, so I escaped it).

I did not really object to the hardships of life at Fettes, and in retrospect I think their effect was beneficial. In other respects, from the start I found it difficult to fit in. It was not so directly a class distinction: my family was middle-class while I suppose many of the others came from upper-class families, but this in itself was hardly noticeable. After all, we wore basically the same clothes, and apart from sweets at the tuck-shop there was nothing to spend money on. However most of the other boys had come through the "prep school" system, so they were used to boarding. They would have had a couple of years of Latin, a subject on which I had had to catch up before sitting the scholarship exam. Much more important, they had been playing rugby for several years already while I only started this at Fettes. If you were not good at rugby, you did not count for much with the other boys; being good in class was actually a disadvantage. (In fact, from arrival at the age of twelve or thirteen, we were always referred to as "men", never "boys"; also, first names were never used – even among ourselves, we called each other by our surnames.)

A major factor in school life was the prefect system. Discipline was not exercised by masters, except in extreme cases: housemasters appointed some of the older boys to be prefects. They were to be addressed as "Sir" and had power to hand out punishments. These could take various forms, mainly dependent on the whim of the prefect concerned: the most usual consisted of having to write out fifty or more lines of Latin in "copperplate" handwriting. A severe breach of rules could lead to a beating: for this the housemaster's permission had to be obtained. On such occasions an ominous silence fell over the entire house: the victim would be led to the changing-room, required to bend over while the assembled prefects lined up to deliver strokes of the cane – usually six.

This happened to me only once, not even for any serious misdemeanour but only because I had accumulated a number of minor ones. I don't think it hurt all that much: worse was the torture-chamber atmosphere of the whole procedure.

If the rules had been reasonable, all this might have been more acceptable. But there were many house rules, plus some school ones. In my house there were about fifty – made up by the prefects, not the housemaster; on arrival the first year, we were given a couple of weeks to learn them, and yet there seemed to be other unwritten rules which a prefect could invoke on the spur of the moment. Many of these rules related to the numerous privileges which prefects enjoyed; having a hot shower in the morning was just one of these. Other offences were trivial, such as walking on the grass instead of staying on the path, or leaving one's jacket unbuttoned, which only prefects were allowed to do.

"Fagging" was part of this system. For the first couple of years, the newest boys were allotted as "fags" – in fact, servants – to the prefects, and had to carry out duties like cleaning their shoes, polishing the buttons on their army uniforms and cleaning their studies. The worst job was lighting the coal fires (there was no other heating): one was supposed to use only part of a fire-lighter, for some reason of economy, and woe betide the fag if the fire failed to light.

Consequently I became increasingly rebellious. Once I invented a long list of ridiculous rules (though not much more so than the official ones) and posted them on the house notice-board. Of course I was found out, and this was serious enough to be dealt with by the housemaster (it was, I think, the only occasion when I had a beating from him, after which one was supposed to say "Thank you sir"). A more subtle act of rebellion consisted of a series of contributions to an unofficial school newsletter called *The Wart*: this was in collaboration with one of my companions in the modern languages class. We called these "Letters to an Aunt" and modelled them on Montesquieu's *Lettres Persanes*. They were a satire on school life; it took some time for the authorities to see the point, but after we had referred to prefects as "gorgeous brutes" action had to be taken and the *Wart* was suspended.[3]

Unsurprisingly, I myself was not appointed a prefect until my last term. Also unsurprisingly, the other prefects shunned me most of the time, as I refused to take part in beatings, avoided giving punishments as much as possible and when necessary tried to invent more constructive tasks, such as learning some poetry. I have to admit that this reforming effort was unsuccessful: on the whole, the culprits preferred to copy out lines of Latin, the traditional punishment.

The prefect system as it was then could be seen, at worst, as a licence for organised bullying, even for sadism. It put excessive power into the hands of youngsters who were not taught how to use it responsibly. One wonders how much this background may be responsible for some of the abuses of colonialism, with "natives" being treated much as small boys at school had been. (This may sound excessive, but when I later read William Golding's *Lord of the Flies* (1954) – a story of schoolboys isolated on their own on an island, who before long turn to savage gang warfare – I felt that I could easily recognise that process.)

At best it could be seen as a preparation for leadership and command, part of the public school role in forming those who would go on to administer, govern and when necessary defend Britain and the Empire. Certainly, in two world wars, officers brought up in this tradition performed valiant service. Fettes had its own war memorial, with long lists for each of the wars, and the annual memorial service was a moving occasion, as the Headmaster read out the "Flanders fields" poem.

Near the end of my period at Fettes, the school had an unusual visit. The French General de Lattre de Tassigny had apparently been much impressed by the performance of British officers and was aware of the public school role in their formation, so he wanted to see for himself. I was given the task of interpreting for him. I don't know how well I performed, but he was very considerate and put me at my ease. He had some of his own staff with him, but for the day I was his aide-de-camp. Naturally, he took particularly interest in the "corps", which put on special demonstrations for him; but he wanted to know about all aspects of our education. That was one of my best days at Fettes.

There is a fitting conclusion to my Fettes experience. My housemaster, H.F. Macdonald, has already been mentioned. As a teacher of Classics (Greek as well as Latin) he probably considered Modern Languages a second-best subject. He liked to tell a story about someone who had a German book which he could not read. "Why not?" one was supposed to ask. "Because", he replied, "the last page was missing, and all the verbs were on that page..." He was no doubt old-fashioned, and I caused him trouble with my rebellious tendencies, but it was his job to uphold the established order and I did not hold that against him. Perhaps over time a certain respect had developed between us. Shortly before the end of my last term, I had a relatively informal talk with him during which he made a surprising remark: "Britain", he said, "has lost its Empire, and has not yet found a role in Europe". Indeed. He might have added that Fettes and other public schools would need to adjust to this situation too – perhaps that was in his mind.[4] But those world events were recent, and the public schools had been around for a long time.

Apart from our excellent modern languages classes, Europe played little role in my Fettes experience. However, my mother – ever vigilant where my education was concerned – arranged for me to have two exchanges during the summer holidays. The first was with a French boy of my age, Michel Guignard. His family lived in Paris, so I was taken to all the usual sights; I particularly enjoyed the Parisian buses with their rear platform – later sadly abolished – and their curious traffic indicators which waved up and down. Then we spent a week at a scout camp on the Loire – very good for my French – followed by a glorious spell in the Midi. The family had a mill-house on a stream near Montpellier: the water was always warm and one could swim at any time. I discovered that figs off the tree were a luscious fruit, nothing like the dried variety I knew; and I was devoured by mosquitoes who obviously appreciated a tender northern skin.

The second exchange – already mentioned – was with a German boy, Günther. He lived with his sister near Hameln (of Pied Piper fame) in a *Schloss* – in fact, something like a large manor-house with extensive farmland. I don't think they had a car – this was in 1948 – but Günther was expert driving a two-horse carriage. I enjoyed this visit too, and practiced my German. But there was something tragic about that household. I don't know what had happened to his parents; Günther had lost an arm, I think in an accident with farm machinery; and he never made the return visit because of some illness. Then I lost touch; many years later I revisited the farm and his sister told me that Günther had died.

After sitting the necessary examination in 1950, I obtained a smallish scholarship to Pembroke College, Cambridge, plus a generous grant from the Kitchener Fund: the latter (it still exists) assists the offspring of former soldiers, especially if they have been wounded, so this was one benefit from my father's wartime service in 1914–18..

Having this under my belt, I was able to take a couple of years off doing various jobs which are not relevant here. More to the point, during those two summers I was tutor to the four boys of an aristocratic French family: the Baron d'Arthuys rented a small but genuine Renaissance château in the *département* of the Creuse.

There I encountered French rural life before farming became mechanised and underwent other big changes. Some cows on the nearby farm were sick: I was told they had *fièvre aphteuse* and was appalled when I found from my dictionary that this was foot-and-mouth disease, which for me meant immediate slaughter of the whole herd – this had at one time been my father's most distasteful task. (Cattle do not necessarily die of the disease but their productivity is much reduced and of course the infection will quickly spread, which is the justification for the UK slaughter policy.)

I also experienced the French concept of good living. Meals were taken around a large family table; there were items of food which I had never known before I was suspicious of artichokes until I found how good they are. I was not yet accustomed to wine and drank water with the meals, but eventually the Baron explained that it was just not possible to eat cheese (a delicious, ripe camembert was always available) without a glass of red wine to go with it. We played *pétanque* on the gravel paths around the château: this has the great advantage over English bowls that it does not require a perfectly smooth grass surface.

The whole family were very kind to me. I reciprocated in two small ways, apart from English lessons. One was with a demonstration to the family and assembled guests of Highland dances – I had brought my kilt with me. The other was to make a minor contribution to the French language. In the afternoons we went to swim in the nearby river, which entailed scrambling over a barbed-wire fence at some risk to limbs and clothing. So I made a stile out of a few pieces of wood. They had never seen this before, and moreover had no word for it, so it was baptised a "Pont Michel" (there is in fact a rarely-used term, *échalier*).

After the rigours of public school life, Cambridge was a pleasant place to spend three years (1952–55). So pleasant, in fact, that some under-graduates hardly bothered to study until almost the last minute before exams. Hardly anyone ever fails those exams: a "Third" denotes very bad performance. Cambridge – like Oxford – has traditionally been a desirable point of passage for gentlemen, as much for social as for educational reasons. Of course both universities also have their traditions of academic excellence. By my time, scholarships were available, and as already mentioned I succeeded in obtaining one, but most undergraduates were there because their parents could afford it. At Cambridge, I was more conscious of wealth disparities than at Fettes: here, there were things to spend money on – in particular, getting the best rooms in college or in private lodgings.

These thoughts are mainly retrospective: at the time, I was too glad to have got there and there was too much to enjoy to bear any such grudges. Most students after arrival spent several months trying to choose between a multitude of activities, sporting or cultural. In the end I settled mainly for music, singing in various choirs. This was a time for the revival of early music. The Dolmetsch family were busy making instruments modelled on ancient instruments: it was said unkindly that if they continued improving their harpsichords they would soon invent the piano, and I remember Carl Dolmetsch coming to demonstrate a triangular model they had just produced, shaped to fit in a London taxi. Another vivid memory is of participating with the university choir in the first performance of Vaughan Williams' *Sea Symphony*: the composer – a very grand old man – was present on the balcony and at the end rose to acknowledge the applause. And to hear evensong in King's College chapel by its superb choir never ceases to be a moving experience.

Spring at Cambridge is a particularly delightful time, with daffodils flowering along the banks of the river (the "backs" – i.e. the areas between several of the colleges and the river Cam). Punts are for hire: one can make leisurely progress downstream between the colleges, or upstream through the countryside. During the summer term the university madrigal society performs from punts on the river; at the end of the concert the punts drift slowly downstream while the choir sings "The Silver Swan". The term concludes with the "May Balls" (which are in June, not in May): these go on all night, and those who are still on their feet by dawn can punt upstream for breakfast in Grantchester.

And if there was any discipline, one hardly noticed it. In my time, college doors closed at ten; until midnight one had to ring the bell for the porter to let you in, and I think one's name was recorded and probably reported to the authorities; maybe if that happened too often there might be some kind of reprimand. Returning after midnight was not really a problem either: each college had some well-known alternative route. At Pembroke this was via a back gate which was not difficult to climb, though the only time I did this I tore my trousers on the spikes. It was rumoured that there was a college – we said in Oxford, but I expect they reversed the compliment – where the night-time passage involved climbing along a branch which overhung the wall, and once inside dropping off on to the roof of a garden shed. When the bursar complained at the cost of constant repairs to the roof, the Fellows after much deliberation solved the problem by having a ladder placed against the branch...

Most of the colleges were for men only; there were just three women's colleges, so girls were in very short supply. Choirs of course required female sopranos, though in chapel choirs the alto parts were often sung by counter-tenors, and there was, as everywhere, a Scottish country dance society with roughly equal numbers. By ten in the evening, visitors of the other sex most definitely had to be out of the college. In at least one of the girls' colleges – Girton, primly situated a couple of miles out of town – a male visitor was not allowed in a woman's room even in daytime unless the bed had been moved into the corridor...

So there were plenty of distractions. Nevertheless, being conscious that I needed a good degree to get on in life, I worked hard. Having gained admittance through languages, I naturally started in the Modern Languages faculty, which after the excellent grounding at Fettes seemed rather easy: I was able to complete the first part of the course in one year, although two could be allowed, and got a good result (II:1). But I found this course rather boring, and the syllabus for Part 2 did not seem very attractive, with studies of minor writers and relatively unimportant periods. So for my second year, more by accident than design, I found myself embarked on Economics Part 2, thereby creating big difficulties for myself. First, I had to catch up on the basics, taught in Part 1. And in any case, the rigour of economic theory was a challenge – in the end, a great benefit – to my hitherto unscientific mind.

Cambridge, of course, had a considerable reputation in economics – the name of Keynes is just the first to come to mind. In my time the lecturing staff included well-known names. Probably the most significant in the theory field was Joan Robinson, whose work on "imperfect competition" was an important corrective to the basic assumption of market equilibrium. But her lectures, consisting largely of complex diagrams on the blackboard, were the most difficult of all to follow. Her husband, Austin Robinson, was more to my taste as his lectures related to current issues: I remember how the day following the presentation in Parliament of the national budget he gave a most lucid analysis of its implications.

In the "Oxbridge" system, attendance at lectures is not obligatory, which is just as well since they do not necessarily correspond to any rationally-designed programme but arise mainly from the personal interests of the lecturers (this is generally true of British universities). Indeed, most of the knowledge required to pass the exams could be obtained from books. More important are the sessions with the personal supervisor, on a one-to-one or perhaps two-to-one basis. On these occasions the supervisor will discuss your last essay, give you the topic for the next one and suggest appropriate reading.

Somehow I struggled through and emerged after my two years of economics with an adequate result (II:2).[5] More important, the unusual combination of languages and economics served me in very good stead. At the time, it was easy enough to find a job after getting one's degree: in fact, in the last summer term, potential employers would come to Cambridge looking for suitable candidates. I was particularly fortunate to be interviewed by Paul Lamartine Yates, who had been asked to recruit a graduate for a post in Geneva with the United Nations. This was to be in the Agriculture Division run jointly by the Food and Agriculture

Organization (headquarters in Rome) and the Economic Commission for Europe in Geneva (not to be confused with the subsequent Commission of the European Communities in Brussels). Yates himself had a distinguished career, in part with the UN, and had written extensively on European agriculture. When I came to write my own first book he gave me valuable advice, so I am doubly indebted to him.

In my last year at Cambridge I shared supervision with a student called John Lebus (it was typical of the system that although he had done relatively little work until just before the finals he got the same grade as I did). He became a good friend, and I owed to him my first visit to Italy. During the last Easter vacation, he and his brother were driving the family car to Florence, where their parents would join them, and they took me there and back.

The impression after crossing the Alps and descending towards Lago Maggiore was unforgettable: suddenly, warmth and colour everywhere. That first evening, after eating in Stresa, we were driving out to our lodging when we were stopped by a policeman – we had forgotten to switch on our headlamps. It was clear that he was going to fine us on the spot. None of us had learnt any Italian; but when the officer wrote down the sum, I remembered musical terminology and said *"Troppo!"* The policeman found this very funny, and we were let off. It was an interesting introduction to easy-going southern ways.

After seeing Florence, I hitch-hiked. This was easier said than done, because at the time many Italians were driving the tiny two-seater Fiat *Topolino* (little mouse); my lifts mostly came from Germans on holiday with large cars (the German recovery must have been well under way by 1955). But I did get to Sienna, Assisi and other places, and came back with a better knowledge of Italian and a great love for the country

---

[1] Since few people have read Part II of Faust, the conclusion of the Faust-Mephistopheles-Gretchen story is little known. After numerous adventures – including an affair with Helen of Troy and a period as Minister of Finance of some undefined country – Faust at last finds fulfilment in what we would now call a rural development project: having used his money to drain a swamp, he looks over a land of happy peasants and pronounces the crucial words of satisfaction which allows Mephisto to claim his soul in reward. Gretchen of course intervenes with a heavenly host to rescue him. I liked to

refer to this much later in life when lecturing on rural development, to the bemusement of my audience.

[2] The role of the "house" and "housemaster" in the public school system needs some explanation. Boys are lodged in several houses; in my time Fettes had six, with about fifty boys in each. The housemaster was *in loco parentis*, responsible for the welfare and moral education of his charges. Also, in principle, for their sex education: this amounted to a single interview, highly embarrassing for both sides, and which seemed to consist of veiled warnings against masturbation ("gentlemen don't do that sort of thing") and an injunction that I must report to him if I saw other boys doing something improper in the toilets (I never did).

[3] My co-conspirator was Bill Kirk, who remained almost the only friend I kept from my Fettes life. At the end of the last year, there was competition for the Governors' Prizes which were awarded one to each subject. As we two were level-pegging, there was a risk that one or other might collect the prizes in both French and German. So we agreed that he would put his effort into German, I into French; and so it worked out. We both got to Cambridge, where he continued with Modern Languages; he became a teacher and in due course headmaster of the international school in Vienna. Very sadly, he died in 1997, soon after his retirement.

[4] Fettes has of course changed, so much so that from its current website it is almost unrecognisable. It started admitting girls in 1981; entrance for UK applicants is now based on the Common Entrance exam, plus interview; scholarships are available which take account of parents' resources; it has admitted foreign students, including several from Eastern Europe; it prepares for the International Baccalaureate, among other certificates; it runs a summer programme on Language and Culture. In fact, it now sounds a rather desirable place.

[5] "Firsts" were rarely granted at Cambridge: in my year in Economics, just two candidates succeeded in this. One was Samuel Brittan, who has been an economic commentator on the *Financial Times* since 1966 and has written interesting books including *Capitalism with a Human Face* (1995). The other was Amartya Sen, who received a Nobel Prize in economics in 1998, has been Master of Trinity College, Cambridge and at the time of writing is a Professor at Harvard.

III. "COLD WAR"
Geneva

By the mid-fifties, the division of Europe had been consolidated. East of the "iron curtain", so-called "democratic" regimes were firmly under the thumb of Moscow. In 1961 the East German regime built the "Berlin Wall" to prevent its citizens passing to the west.

The armies of NATO and the Warsaw Pact faced each other across the divide. The USSR had tested its first atom bomb in 1949, Britain a year later and France in 1960.

Economic recovery in Western Europe had been greatly aided by the Marshall Plan (former General George Marshall was the US Secretary of State), under which from 1947 till 1951 the USA provided economic and technical assistance. This had been offered also to the USSR and its allies but they did not accept it.

Membership of the Organisation for European Economic Cooperation (OEEC), set up in Paris to administer the Marshall Plan, was confined to the United States and Western Europe plus Greece and Turkey.[1] However, the UN Economic Commission for Europe (ECE), established in Geneva by the United Nations, also in 1947, in principle covered all Europe. Its mandate too was to help in rebuilding post-war Europe, to develop economic activity and to strengthen economic relations between European countries and between them and the other countries of the world.

However, the political division of Europe forced the ECE to deal only with questions that were of common interest, and the Soviet side took a narrow view of what that could mean. The top economics staff of the secretariat in the mid-1950s included some big names, and their annual report on the state of the European economy was highly regarded, though the secretariat's influence on policy was minimal. Meetings of the member countries consisted mainly of a series of national statements. There was some exchange of information and the secretariat produced statistical reports which tried as far as possible to cover all Europe. Probably the ECE's most useful activity – which continues – has been to establish standards for internationally-traded agricultural products, many of which were later taken on by the European Economic Community.[2]

The secretariat included an Agriculture Division, which was partly staffed by the Food and Agriculture Organization (FAO) in Rome. It was to this that I was appointed, as a statistical assistant. As already mentioned, I had no talent for mathematics, and my Cambridge economics course had not included any training in statistics. However, I bought a "teach-yourself" book and found that statistics didn't require advanced mathematical skills but rather a systematic handling of basic data. We had calculating machines – rather like a big office typewriter, with a carriage which clanked along as it churned out the results; I also made extensive use of a slide-rule. In the present computer age, those methods must seem hopelessly antiquated, yet they had their advantages, calling for a greater awareness of magnitudes; electronic calculators make it too easy. And I have always been sceptical about the precision of most economic data.

The Division was headed by a Frenchman, Pierre Sinard, for whom I developed a great respect. (Later, when the Commission of the European Economic Community was being established in Brussels, he was a candidate for the post of Director-General of Agriculture, but the post went to another Frenchman, Louis Rabot.)

He soon gave me interesting tasks. The first was to prepare a report on the trends in the horse population in European countries. This was a more important topic than it might seem. With mechanisation, the number of working farm-horses was in decline: that in turn meant less land would be needed to grow fodder, oats in particular, so more land could be released to produce foodstuffs for humans. The task was to collect as much information as possible and to project future trends. One econometric tool for this, with data showing the age distribution of a population, was the "Markov chain", which I could use in a simple way to work out year-by-year how many of each age group were likely to remain. Pierre Sinard took time and trouble to explain this and other matters to me. Another very helpful senior member of the Division was Denis Britton, who became Professor of Agricultural Economics at Nottingham University, then at Wye Agricultural College in Kent; in fact, when he retired in 1985 I filled his post there for a year until a more permanent replacement could be made.

Then the Division became involved with FAO in Rome in a large-scale study to project food supply and demand. This gave me the opportunity to go several times to Rome to co-operate with staff there. The FAO building has a restaurant-terrace with a fine view overlooking the Terme de Caracalla. In October 1956 I was there with my FAO colleague, a Frenchman named Louis Goreux, when news came through of the Anglo-French invasion at Suez: we were both appalled.

Those research tasks went well beyond my job description. In fact, I had been recruited at the top level of the "general" grades, whereas with a degree I should have been at the first "professional" grade. This did not initially bother me: in any case, the salary seemed astronomical by British standards. But there was a career problem: UN agencies have to maintain a reasonable balance between nationalities, and the British "quota" was seriously overfilled. (I even thought of applying for Irish nationality, to which I would have been entitled in view of my father's origins.)

Then an unexpected event occurred. In October 1956 the Hungarian people rose against their Communist regime. After some hesitation in Moscow, Soviet tanks were sent in; there was fierce fighting in the streets of Budapest; some 20,000 citizens were killed. The international community reacted feebly. Britain and France were absorbed with their fruitless invasion of Suez; American media seemed at one stage to encourage the revolt, but no help was forthcoming. As the repression continued, many Hungarians fled into Austria, some into Yugoslavia.

The Office of the High Commissioner for Refugees (UNHCR) slowly moved into action. This was also situated in Geneva, at the other end of the *Palais des Nations* from the ECE. They needed extra staff, and I was recruited as a statistical officer (in the "professional" category this time) as part of a small unit whose job was to keep count of the refugees: figures were urgently required so that the necessary assistance could be planned.

Easier said than done: the surge across the frontiers had been sudden and unexpected and no accurate counts had been made. Moreover, some so-called "old" Hungarian refugees who had been stranded in camps since 1945 with little hope of ever getting out had seen an opportunity, going back into Hungary and then returning as "new" refugees. One had to make estimates trying to reconcile arrivals, numbers in camps, those put on trains to other Western European countries, etc. Mysteriously, some trains arrived at destination with more than the recorded number on departure, others with less. It was a very confused situation. We were still trying to make sense of it when a "final" figure was demanded: I gave as my best estimate 190,000. Later information indicated this was probably about 10,000 too high, but the first figure had stuck. I don't know whether subsequently people were still looking for the missing 10,000. (I see now that the figure usually quoted is 200,000.)

The Hungarian refugee problem was the biggest crisis the UNHCR had faced in Europe since its inception – later, alas, there were far bigger numbers to cope with in other parts of the world and I am sure it has become a very different organisation.[3] In 1956/57, I did not feel it was coping very well. The staff was too small to manage an event of this kind; moreover, many of its staff were officials left over from the pre-war

League of Nations, with no particular competence. I became increasingly frustrated by what I saw as inefficiency in the face of an urgent need. A turning-point came when I found that in the midst of it all one of our financial controllers was carrying out a lengthy and detailed investigation into some cracked toilet bowls in a Yugoslav refugee camp. There was clearly no future for me in the UNHCR, though I suppose that, had I stayed, more interesting and certainly lucrative positions might have opened up within the UN system. But I was young and idealistic, and I quit.

For an academic year I followed an excellent diploma course at the Graduate Institute of International Studies in Geneva: this was taught by Professor Wilhelm Röpke and dealt with the analysis of national budgets.[4] It had much more relevance to the real world than anything I had received at Cambridge. And I earned some money translating articles from, of all things, a bulletin published by a German cosmetics firm, for which I had to acquire a specialised chemical vocabulary.

In the meantime, European integration was making its first tentative steps, and a new opportunity arose.

---

[1] The Treaty of Versailles in 1919 had imposed on defeated Germany both humiliating conditions and punitive reparations, which contributed to the rise of Nazism. At least that lesson of history had been learnt. On the part of the United States, the Marshall Plan was generous but it was also in the US interest that Western Europe should recover as quickly as possible (and that it should not fall to communist revolutions). It was never likely that the US Congress would endorse expenditure for Soviet-supported regimes: conditions attached to the aid made it unlikely that they would accept.

[2] As the work of ECE (Geneva) is little known, it is worth quoting its current website:

"For more than 40 years, ECE was the only instrument of economic dialogue and cooperation between two radically different systems, and it may legitimately be proud of the results achieved in such a difficult context including the network of 'E' roads linking all European countries, the harmonization of road signs and signals, safety and anti-pollution standards for motor vehicles, standards for the transport of dangerous goods by road, the agreement for the development of combined transport, standards for perishable agricultural produce, agreements on customs procedures and various trade regulations, standards for the electronic exchange of trade and transport data and conventions on transboundary air pollution, the protection of water, courses and the transboundary effects of industrial accidents. At the same time, its analyses and statistics on regional economic development are considered authoritative."

[3] The UNHCR website says:
"In more than five decades, the agency has helped an estimated 50 million people restart their lives. Today, a staff of around 6,300 people in more than 110 countries continues to help 31.7 million persons."

[4] Wilhelm Röpke (1899-1966) deserves to be better known in anglophone circles. During the depression of the 1930s, he came to conclusions similar to those of Keynes. He spoke out against Nazism, and left Germany in 1933; he held his post in Geneva from 1937 until his death. He was an adviser to the post-war German Federal Government and was one of the leading exponents of the "social market economy". There is an excellent Internet article – www.thefreemanonline.org/featured/wilhelm-ropke-a-centenary-appreciation.

IV. EUROPEAN INTEGRATION –
FIRST STEPS
London and Paris

In 1950 the French foreign minister, Robert Schuman, proposed the creation of a single authority to control the production of coal and steel in France and West Germany, as a way to prevent further war between the two. The proposal was realised in the European Coal and Steel Community including, besides France and Germany, Belgium, Luxembourg, the Netherlands and Italy.

In 1957 the same six countries signed the Treaty of Rome, establishing the European Economic Community (comprising the "common market"), which came into force on 1 January 1958.

Britain had declined to participate in the Messina conference in 1955 at which the EEC project was launched.[1] Instead, Britain took the initiative in setting up the European Free Trade Association with Austria, Denmark, Norway, Portugal, Sweden and Switzerland (enabling journalists to coin the phrase "Europe at Sixes and Sevens"). EFTA did not have a common external tariff nor a common agricultural policy.

Although Britain stood apart from the negotiations among the Six, those developments were seen as having considerable importance. Consequently, a London research institute, Political and Economic Planning (PEP), embarked on a range of studies into the implications for Britain and recruited a team for this purpose. I was appointed as a research assistant to work on agricultural policy, under the direction of Ted Lloyd, who as already mentioned had been an Under-Secretary in the Ministry of Food.

Major obstacles to British participation in the European Economic Community (EEC) – apart from the political awkwardness of joining a club led by France and Germany – lay in its plans for a common external tariff and a common agricultural policy. Britain had a long tradition of free trade, extending to agricultural products. As this meant cheap foodstuffs – good for consumers but not for farmers – the latter were supported by a unique system of "deficiency payments", making up the difference between the market price and a guaranteed price for each main product.

My main task in PEP was therefore to follow the preparations being made by the EEC for a common agricultural policy. The Treaty of Rome had defined the general objectives and the principles were developed at the Stresa Conference in July 1958. The Commission – responsible under the Treaty for proposing policy to the Council of Ministers – had a vital role to play in this as in other aspects. Besides the strong personality of its first President, Walter Hallstein (German), it had a dynamic team for agriculture in the persons of the Commissioner, Sicco Mansholt (Dutch), the Director-General for Agriculture, Louis Rabot (French) and the Deputy-Director-General for markets, Heringa (Dutch).

Since each of the six Member States had over the years developed a variety of support mechanisms for farmers, and there was no question of removing this support, the institution of a common market meant somehow merging these measures into a "common agricultural policy" (CAP). Inevitably, in view of pressure from the farm unions, there was a strong tendency on the part of the Member States to align prices upwards rather than downwards, which implied a substantial degree of protection at the common frontier.

Over the couple of years I spent at PEP, we produced a series of "Occasional Papers" explaining Commission proposals and analysing their implications for Britain in particular. The Commission, of course, was working mainly in French, so these were the first such studies in English. (Many years later, while I was in my post in Brussels, a young journalist asked me how long I had been working on the CAP. When I replied "Well, since before it existed", he could hardly have looked more surprised if I said I had been present at the creation of the world...).

The key issues were the levels at which prices of farm products would be supported within the EEC, and the mechanisms for doing so. The Commission did not seek a highly protective system, but had to take account of political realities. Germany had, on the whole, the highest prices. France – often blamed for the subsequent excesses of the CAP – could have accepted lower levels, knowing its big grain producers would have a competitive advantage; the Netherlands had the lowest price levels. Inevitably, in view of pressure from farm organisations, the target prices finally agreed were closer to the German levels. The complex mechanisms incorporated features from previous policies in each of the Member States: in particular, market intervention by public bodies (deriving mainly from French practice) and variable import levies (from Germany, indeed from former Nazi policies). All this was in stark contrast to British priorities, and seemed to make the prospect of British membership even more remote.

Another important issue was "Commonwealth preference" (formerly "Imperial preference"). Under this scheme the Commonwealth countries were supposed to grant preferential tariffs on their imports from each other. Its existence was another reason why Britain was so reluctant to join the EEC: applying the common external tariff would mean the end of Commonwealth preference. But was it really so important? I proposed a study, but my superiors in PEP were not interested. So I did this on my own, mainly out of office hours and at home. It was a big task, which involved going through the UK tariff and trade statistics, and applying the degree of preference to the value of trade in each item. When I produced the result, which confirmed that the preferences granted by the UK were not very significant except for some products, PEP grudgingly agreed to publish it. I do not know how much effect this had, but the issue of Commonwealth preference did gradually fade away.[2]

Most people thought it unlikely that Britain would seek or obtain membership of the EEC in the foreseeable future, largely because of the agricultural policy issue. It was not so much a problem for British farmers, though the National Farmers' Union was protesting loudly: despite the much-reduced number of farmers (about 5% of the population at the time) the NFU was a powerful lobby. In fact, farmers would hardly have suffered under the EEC's high-price regime. Nor, as seen above, was Commonwealth preference such a big issue, apart from specific products which could probably be handled individually. The big problem would be the rise in food prices to consumers.

But the prospect of Western Europe remaining indefinitely at "Sixes and Sevens" seemed unpalatable. An article I wrote for the *Westminster Bank Review* (February 1961), entitled "Agriculture and a European Economic Union", suggested possible ways in which these food and agriculture issues might be resolved. In fact I was much too optimistic: as later events showed, the Six were not prepared to make exceptions to the rules of its common agricultural policy.

All this was interesting and quite important, but in PEP I had soon found that I was expected to do all the work, while my supervisor, Ted Lloyd, occasionally looked in but took all the credit. (I realised subsequently that this is standard civil service practice; of course, his name was still known in Whitehall and probably added status to our publications.) As for the "Commonwealth preference" study, I had done this entirely on my own, yet my name appeared only in small print. Moreover, all the young research staff were poorly paid; we were expected to be grateful for the "experience". So when in 1960 an opening appeared in Paris, I jumped at it.

The OEEC, having fulfilled its mandate to administer the Marshall Plan, was converted in 1961 into the OECD – Organisation for Economic Co-operation and Development – with the United States and Canada as full members. There were originally twenty member countries. Japan, then Australia and New Zealand joined in the 1960s.[3]

Its stated task was (and is) to help its member countries to achieve sustainable economic growth and employment and to contribute to the development of the world economy. Having no money to hand out – it is itself financed by contributions from its members – it can do this only through its reports and by providing a forum for consultation between the member countries.

My OECD appointment was to its Agricultural Policies Division. This unit had been making annual reports on agricultural policy in each member country, a practice which continued for a few more years. The Division was quite small, so each of us got three or four countries to work on; the allocation was usually changed each year, so that after a while we each came to know most of the countries concerned.

When these annual reports became repetitious, we switched to making studies of specific issues. Our work programme had to be approved by the relevant committee of member countries, but in practice the Secretariat's suggestions usually went through. Over the thirteen years I spent in this Division, our reports included the agricultural development problems of Southern European countries, the economic implications of food aid, projections of world agricultural supply and demand (to 1975 and 1985) and other matters.

Throughout this period, my immediate superior was Albert Simantov, a Greek of immense ability combined with great kindness and modesty; we both got promotions, so that he ended up (somewhat reluctantly) as Director for Agriculture while I became head of the Agricultural Policies Division. The working atmosphere was always excellent: besides staff members from several Western European countries, my Division had an American and – as the OECD membership expanded – a Japanese and an Australian, each adding to the variety and interest of the work.

Working on different countries and new topics was stimulating; it also gave an incentive to learn something of the language of the country in question. It was customary to visit the relevant agricultural ministry to obtain information and to discuss the draft report. One advantage of working on agriculture is that "field visits" are always interesting, and one gets to know a little about farming in various contexts; I found that my counterparts in those ministries were always happy to arrange such trips in the course of a visit.

This was even more the case when our work moved increasingly into rural development issues. I remember in particular a week in Turkey at a time when a new development plan was being prepared. After discussions in Ankara, I was taken northwards to the Black Sea, along the coast, then inland to Erzerum, with many discussions along the way with local authorities and farmers. On this and other occasions, I was struck by the great contrasts in Turkish society between an educated, cosmopolitan elite and the mass of the peasantry (still well over half the population). On one occasion a man working alone in a field got quite angry when I wanted to take a photo. Later, in the countryside near Erzerum, I noticed a group of women washing clothes in a stream: it was a picturesque scene with their colourful clothing, so I asked if I could take a photo. After some consultation and giggling, the message that came back through my interpreter was that their men-folk would not like it, but since none of them were there, the women had no objection…

A quite different mission took me round the world: this was just after Australia and New Zealand had joined OECD. I had some business in Washington, then flew via Los Angeles – with a welcome stop-over in Tahiti – to Wellington. I spent a week in New Zealand, going north to Auckland and south to Dunedin, talking to experts and visiting farms. Then I had a week in Australia, with a similar programme. In each country I was also on a recruiting mission for a staff member for my Agricultural Policies Division, and in Australia found an excellent candidate who joined us soon afterwards and made a valuable contribution to our work.

The accession of Japan had already brought a most interesting new dimension to our work. The Japanese Ministry of Agriculture provided one of their experts to work with us: Seiji Shindo. He became one of our best colleagues and also did much to introduce us to Japanese culture. One result was that in 1971 I took extended leave to spend a long summer as a Visiting Professor at Kyoto University, taking my family along. Besides lecturing on European agriculture to staff and senior students, I embarked on a study of Japanese agricultural policy, on which there was very little information in any other language.

This work was supported both by the universities and by the Ministry of Agriculture, so I had very privileged tours taking me both to Kyushu in the south and Hokkaido in the north. Cultural differences made it quite difficult to gather precise information: Japanese do not like to commit themselves individually to give an answer which might be wrong and cause them to lose face; they much prefer to discuss among themselves and give a collective answer. Even then, it was often so vague that I would have to check it with another group. On the other hand, their habit of working as a group had advantages: in the Ministry of Agriculture in Tokyo there was one official responsible for organising my tours, but if he was not there when I phoned there would always be someone else who knew all about it. The results of my investigations were published by the Trade Policy Centre in London.[4]

From this and a later, private visit, I came to have great admiration for the best aspects of Japanese culture, so different from our own. One notable feature, related to their respect for tradition and for their elders, is the emphasis on "schools" in each artistic or intellectual sphere. At the end of my stay at Kyoto University, some of the staff said they had found my lectures interesting, but they had a problem: to what "school" did I belong? I said I had never thought about that: I tried to teach the facts as I found them. Anyway, they decided among themselves that I belonged to the "historical" economic school, a solution which satisfied everyone.

Returning to OECD: I think the quality of our reports was high. OECD in general promoted liberal economic policies, and we generally stressed the adverse effects of agricultural protectionism and high price supports. However, OECD has no power over the policies of its Member States. Our reports were discussed at meetings with delegates from the various agricultural ministries, most of whom tried to tone down our recommendations as much as possible. Soon we were having considerable difficulty with whoever was representing the European Commission: the shape which the common agricultural policy was taking was not at all in line with our relatively academic ideas. Of course, the agricultural exporters among the Member States, particularly the USA (despite its own very supportive policies) and later Australia and New Zealand, used these meetings as an opportunity to attack EEC protectionism, to little effect.

In fact, in due course I began to feel that the OECD was outliving its usefulness, in the agricultural policy sphere at least, with meetings increasingly dominated by this cleavage between the two groups of countries. When Britain, Ireland and Denmark joined the European Community in 1973, this dichotomy was bound to be accentuated.

I personally felt the time had come to move on again. As a result of my visit to Australia, I was offered a tempting post in the Department of Primary Industry in Canberra. However, opportunities were also opening up in Brussels. My choice of the latter had less to do with the characteristics of the job than with the feeling that, after all, my place was in Europe.

> *Once it was clear that the European Economic Community was not going to collapse, the British government opened negotiations for entry. Two attempts – in which Britain was seeking various concessions – were vetoed by President de Gaulle. In its third attempt, when Georges Pompidou had replaced de Gaulle, Britain accepted the "acquis communautaire" (the whole body of EEC law) subject only to temporary derogations: this succeeded, and Britain – together with Ireland and Denmark – joined the Community in January 1973.*

The story of Britain's relations with the European Community is long and tortuous, and has formed the subject of many books; it need not be retold here. Being in Paris between 1960 and 1973, I observed the process as much from the French side as the British. Objectively, the British position was weak: they had contributed nothing to the formation of the Community, and on the contrary were widely suspected of having tried to torpedo it, particularly by setting up EFTA instead.

And of course, British negotiators encountered an immovable obstacle in the person of de Gaulle. There was much justification for his obstinacy. Partly this must have been due to resentment at his treatment by Churchill and Roosevelt during the war: reading his *Mémoires de Guerre*, it seemed as if he had spent more time arguing with his allies than fighting the Germans. And he was always passionately patriotic: when in his speeches he referred to *"La France "* or *"la patrie"*, the words vibrated with emotion (try doing the same with "the United Kingdom" or even "Great Britain").

France, after its defeat in 1940, needed a great leader, as Britain needed Churchill, and de Gaulle provided this by his wartime role as well as by his firmness in 1961 when he quashed the revolt by the generals in Algeria. On that occasion we heard tanks rumbling into Paris, without being quite sure which side they were on, and I remember the broadcast speech in which de Gaulle forebade the troops to obey the rebel generals. He was indeed an eloquent speaker, and his televised press conferences were great occasions. Like Churchill, he stayed on too long, until the revolts of May 1968 demonstrated that he had lost touch with the younger generations and with the workers. But a visit to his home, now a museum, at Colombey-les-Deux-Eglises, and to his simple tomb in the village churchyard, is a moving experience.

De Gaulle's opposition to British overtures had less to do with the technicalities of the EEC negotiations than with basic political principles. He had not forgotten that Churchill had declared to him that if Britain had to choose between Europe and *"le grand large"* (i.e. principally her

American ally) she would always choose the latter. And it was widely reported that in 1967, rejecting the conditions Britain was seeking in its second application, he had said: *"L'Angleterre, je la veux nue..."* (he denied this, amusingly but unconvincingly, at his subsequent press conference).

His successor, Georges Pompidou, had fewer objections of principle, while Prime Minister Edward Heath's success in getting agreement was largely due to his strong European commitment, and perhaps too his apparent lack of enthusiasm for the American "special relationship". The key passage of their agreement in May 1971 stated:

"The President of the Republic and the British Prime Minister established that their views on the role and development of Europe are in all essentials identical. They noted the importance of Franco-German reconciliation as a foundation for the European Communities. They agreed that ... it was their joint interest and common purpose to develop the enlarged Community as a basis for the growing unity of Europe."

It was also stated, among other crucial matters, that the European Community would not replace member nations but would create a new framework for them; and that while the Commission would continue to make "a valuable contribution", the Council of Ministers must remain the forum for taking decisions: this should have reassured those who feared a federal union. Heath had also endorsed the "Luxembourg compromise", under which it was understood that if a Member State declared a "vital interest" on a particular point, it could not be voted down, whatever Treaty provisions said: this was a matter on which de Gaulle had nearly caused the EEC to break down.

The leaders confirmed the results of ongoing negotiations, to the effect that "Community preference" would take the place of "Commonwealth preference" and that Britain would adopt the common agricultural policy with only temporary derogations: in fact, Britain had given in to insistence on the EEC side that new members must accept the existing body of legislation (the *acquis communautaire*).

In a further concession to French sensitivities, Heath had agreed that British officials appointed to the European institutions would be able to work in French, and that efforts would be made to improve the knowledge of French in Britain; there was no reciprocal undertaking as regards English.

The content of this agreement was kept secret: it is questionable whether if the extent of his concessions had been known, Heath could have got the legislation through his Parliament. Indeed, as subsequent events were to prove, Edward Heath was speaking more for himself than for the country at large.[5] One could argue as to whether that was an act of far-sighted statesmanship or a flagrant disregard for democratic procedures. That issue, however, belongs to the next chapter.

---

[1] As the institutions have changed over time, so have their titles, and this is confusing. From 1958 there were three institutions: the European Coal and Steel Community, the European Atomic Energy Community ("Euratom") and the European Economic Community (EEC). In 1967 they were merged into the "European Communities", with a single Commission and Council of Ministers; this entity was in practice often referred to in the singular as "The European Community". The often-used term "Common Market" does not refer to an institution but to one of the main elements of the EEC. Further to confuse matters, following the Maastricht Treaty, the European Community became the "European Union" (EU) in 1993.

All this makes for awkwardness in any writing on the history of European integration. I have used one or other of these terms depending on the context.

[2] As this matter of Commonwealth preference has some historical significance, and as my report has been long out-of-print, the main results are reproduced below.

UK IMPORTS FROM THE COMMONWEALTH, 1957

	Value of imports	Average percentage margin of preference	
	£ million	on goods enjoying preference	on all goods
Food, beverages, tobacco	722	8	6
Raw materials	702	8	2
Mineral fuels	189	13	0
Manufactured goods	146	16	12
Miscellaneous	11	0	0
Total imports	1769	9	4

[3] By the present time (2009), the inclusion of Central/Eastern countries has taken the total membership of OECD to thirty; further expansion is envisaged, possibly including Russia and non-European countries including India, China, Indonesia, Brazil, Chile and others.

[4] My study resulting from this time in Japan was entitled *Japanese Agriculture at the Crossroads* (Trade Policy Research Centre, London, 1972). Japan's agricultural policy turned around rice: heavily subsidised and protected by a virtual import ban, it was produced on very small holdings mainly by part-time farmers. I made suggestions for changes in policy, but I don't think any of them were ever applied. Support to rice producers was always important to the ruling Liberal-Democratic party.

[5] The minutes of the meeting between Heath and Pompidou are now available on Internet (see www.margaretthatcher.org/archive). That organisation probably resurrected them as proof of Heath's perfidy; one can also draw the opposite conclusion and consider that he showed far-sighted statesmanship.

V. THE EUROPEAN UNION
Brussels – Council of Ministers

In 1973, Denmark, Ireland and the United Kingdom became full members of the European Community, accepting the Treaty of Rome and subsequent legislation (the "acquis communautaire") with only transitional derogations. This meant, above all, that they became part of the "common market" – meaning free movement of goods between the Member States and a common system of protection (import duties etc.) in respect of goods from the rest of the world. It also meant that they would receive benefits from and contribute to the Community budget.

Of the Community institutions, the biggest in terms of staff is the Commission; there is also the Council of Ministers and the European Parliament, each with its secretariat; likewise the Economic and Social Committee. The European Court of Justice is responsible for interpreting and ensuring respect for Community legislation.

NB: Some of the institutional arrangements described here have been modified by the Lisbon Treaty, which is discussed in Chapter IX.

The Treaty of Rome established a unique institutional structure, unparalleled in any nation-state – which is probably why it is so often misunderstood. Most people know about the Commission, if only because its Berlaymont building in Brussels is conspicuous and architecturally interesting (its X-shaped structure is suspended from its frame rather than being built up from below). Basically, the Commission's job is to prepare legislation and propose it to the Council of Ministers, and subsequently to implement whatever measures are decided. The Council, where all Member States are represented, did not initiate policy but had the ultimate power of decision on Commission proposals. In general, it had to consult the European Parliament, but at the time of which I am writing this was usually a formality. It was also supposed to consult the Economic and Social Committee, but paid even less attention to the opinions from this quarter.

The Council of Ministers usually met in the Charlemagne building, next to the Berlaymont; proximity between the two institutions is important since Commission officials may be called at very short notice to appear at meetings of the Council and its dependent committees and working parties.[1] Nevertheless, in October, April and June the Council had to meet in Luxembourg, which caused many practical problems, requiring staff – especially translators – to be on hand just in case they were needed. The invention of the fax – I remember the very first faxed message arriving from Brussels – and later no doubt of e-mail greatly helped to solve such problems.

The Treaty (on French insistence) also required sessions of the Parliament to be held in Strasbourg, while its Secretariat was then mostly in Luxembourg. The inconvenience and expense of this arrangement, in particular the van-loads of documents that have to be transported, is notorious. It is also much disliked by the members of the European Parliament, as Strasbourg has relatively few airline connections.

With the accession agreement, nationals of Denmark, Ireland and the United Kingdom could be recruited to the Community institutions. In my post in OECD in Paris as Head of the Agricultural Policies Division, I had worked with several officials in the Commission's Directorate-General for Agriculture. A particularly close contact was with Raymond Craps, who headed a Directorate covering both "socio-structural" policy and economic analysis; I was also on good terms with Louis Rabot, the Director-General. It was understood between us that the Directorate would be divided into two, and that I would be put in charge of economics.

The British civil service, however, had other ideas, and in practice appointments to senior posts in the European institutions were controlled by the national authorities. So I was called for interview in London. Only one item really mattered. After some general discussion, a question was put which went roughly like this: "Well, Mr Tracy: we know that as a European official you are expected to be impartial... however, supposing an issue were to arise where British interests were particularly concerned, what would be your attitude...?" I fear that my answer did not satisfy them.

In any case, it did not really matter: as I realised later, an official from the British Ministry of Agriculture was already lined up for the Commission job.[2] Instead, I was offered a post as a Director in the Secretariat of the Council of Ministers. Like most people, I knew little about this body. The Council Secretariat was not provided for in the Treaty of Rome but grew up out of necessity: a secretariat was required to organise meetings and above all to make reports from one session to another. So, as I soon discovered, members of the Secretariat spend most of their time sitting in meetings, taking notes and subsequently writing up the necessary reports. As meetings may follow each other in quick succession, this has to be done quickly, the more so since the reports must immediately go to the Secretariat's translation services to be rendered into all the official languages. The practice at the time was for all reports to be drafted in French, which simplified the translation arrangements.

All this is a very necessary task and the Secretariat handles it efficiently. A good report that highlights the main issues and groups countries according to their positions can greatly facilitate the next stage of discussions. Some meetings are recorded, but usually the Secretariat staff rely on their meeting notes. They are not supposed to speak at meetings, as I discovered early on when in a working party I reverted to OECD habits and gave my views on whatever was under discussion: the Danish chairman afterwards made it clear to me, politely but firmly, that this was not my job.

In principle, the Secretariat is available to advise the various chairmen if so required: this is usually done verbally, but for ministerial sessions, written briefs are prepared on each item on the agenda. In this way the Secretariat can help considerably to advance the negotiations, particularly by keeping in touch with the various delegations, and with the Commission services, so that the President can be prepared for their probable positions. However, the Council Presidency changes every six months, and this applies to all committees and working parties as well as to the ministerial Councils. So the Secretariat is constantly working for different masters. Some do appreciate the available advice; others – particularly Ministers – may rush into meetings with no time for previous briefing. On the whole, delegates from the larger countries are more likely to rely on their own national services. Sometimes the Secretariat can only look on in dismay as a President launches into a fruitless course which its advice could have averted.

The Council Presidency

The Presidency's task is primarily to chair all meetings – not just the Council of Ministers but all committees and working-parties, where the chairpersons are drawn from their national representations in Brussels or from their home civil service. It determines the agenda for each meeting: in practice this is proposed by the Secretariat taking into account the proposals received from the Commission and the state of the negotiations, but the Presidency has some leeway to promote items in which it is particularly interested or to defer others.

The six-monthly rotation of the Presidency made some sense in the Community of Six, when each country got a turn every four years, and with time would have experience to draw upon. With nine Member

States, it still did not work too badly. The main merit of the system is the temporary prestige conferred on the presiding country, particularly the smaller ones who for their term of office have had the task of managing the Community's affairs and – together with the Commission – representing it internationally.

The main drawback is that each country arrives in the post with its own agenda, which it usually does not have time to carry out. And of course, some countries are better at the job than others. This does not necessarily mean that big countries are more efficient than small ones. On the contrary, they are more inclined to use their Presidency to promote their own objectives; from the Secretariat's point of view, they are more difficult to work with because they rely more on their own experts. At the other extreme, little Luxembourg was usually an excellent Presidency: remarkably efficient despite the small staff at its disposal, and usually much more objective in pursuing Community priorities.

Of course, there are big differences between individual presidents, at all levels. Among those who chaired the ministerial Council during my period in the Secretariat, some stand out in my memory. Josef Ertl, the German Minister of Agriculture from 1969 till 1982, was a bluff Bavarian who would fight for his farming constituency every inch of the way. As President, diplomacy was not his style. While a Minister was in the chair, his country's spokesman would be a deputy Minister or perhaps the top civil servant, but this would not deter Ertl from pursuing, perhaps not the interests of the German farmers, but at any rate those of farmers in general – which would bring him into conflict particularly with the British, for whom the farming interest was secondary.[3] Negotiations could drag on over successive meetings and agreement still seem far away. Yet Ertl also knew the importance of the whole European project: ultimately, just as breakdown seemed imminent, he would produce some concession – just enough to get discussion going again, and finally, with everyone exhausted, a compromise agreement would be reached.

The best president I knew was Kostas Simitis, who became Greek Minister of Agriculture in 1981. With a strong academic background in both law and economics, he was intelligent, fair and quite un-Greek in main-taining his calm in all circumstances. I was not surprised when he became Prime Minister in 1996, and he did a good deal to stabilise the Greek economy. He withdrew from politics in 2004, having other priorities.

Another excellent president was Michel Rocard, French Minister of Agriculture in 1983-85, likewise competent and objective in his role. He too later became a Prime Minister, but subsequently did not play as big a role in French politics as he deserved and as France perhaps needed. Maybe intelligence and fairness are not the best assets in national politics.

I have a less favourable memory of Jacques Chirac, whose first ministerial post was in agriculture in 1972-74. I recollect in particular how after delivering his prepared speech he would read his papers while other ministers were speaking – an unusual discourtesy in the Council chamber. But he was already an astute politician, well able to manipulate the French farm lobby in his favour. I have never been able to see in Chirac much more than a very successful showman. When he attained his presidential ambition, the "body language" of his press conferences, with wide sweeping gestures, was obviously modelled on that of de Gaulle.[4]

Undoubtedly the worst French agriculture minister of this time was Edith Cresson (1981-83), appointed by Francois Mitterrand. She knew little about agriculture or the issues of the day and was obviously dependent on briefs from her officials. Even then her interventions were pitiful – my Greek student at the College of Europe who had represented France at one of our "simulations" of the Council negotiations (see later chapter) would have done a better job. Fortunately, Cresson was never in the presidential chair. But later she became Prime Minister under Mitterrand – she did not last long – and then a Commissioner in Brussels. In the latter role she is mainly remembered for giving very remunerative contracts to individuals – including her dentist – whose qualifications were dubious.

Agricultural policy

The Treaty of Rome had laid down the main principles of a common agricultural policy. This was a key element in forming the European Economic Community. In particular, France - a major agricultural exporter – saw this as a necessary counterpart to the advantages which Germany's manufacturing sector would gain from the Common Market. But all the member countries supported and protected their farmers in various ways: there was no question of permitting free competition in agricultural products unless some such support continued to be provided. By 1962 the Six had agreed on various measures to support internal agricultural markets and on protection against imports mainly by a system of import levies.

When I arrived in Brussels in mid-1973 in the Secretariat's Agriculture Directorate-General, I was first struck by the importance of agriculture in the work of the European Community institutions – in OECD it received low priority, so that the agricultural services were the first to be banished to outlying premises when rebuilding was under way. But in Brussels, the CAP was seen as a vital ingredient; indeed, by 1973 support for farmers was absorbing two-thirds of the Community budget. The Commission's

Agriculture Directorate-General (DGVI) was one of the biggest. Overall, the Council Secretariat is much smaller than the Commission, but there too the Agriculture Directorate-General was one of the largest.

Ministers of Agriculture met in Council once a month (except in August); the Special Committee for Agriculture (SCA) which prepared its meetings met on Mondays and Tuesdays every week except when there was a Council session; and meetings of specialised working parties went on constantly. Only the "General" Council, attended usually by Foreign Ministers, met as often as their agricultural colleagues. The significance of the Agriculture Council was also underlined by the fact that it had the "Special" Committee to prepare its sessions; this was attended normally by senior officials from the various ministries of agriculture, and by the top officials in the Commission's DGVI. Other Council formations are served by the Committee of Permanent Representatives (COREPER).

The Agriculture Council was notorious for its "marathon" sessions. These usually occurred at the end of March each year, at the climax of the annual "price-fixing" negotiations. The guaranteed price for milk had to be decided by 1 April, otherwise there would be a legal void, with potentially disastrous consequences; and as a "package" was the only way to reach a compromise acceptable to all delegations, in practice the support arrangements for all major commodities had to be settled by the same date. The Commission submitted its proposals well in advance, probably in January, but most delegations would not make any significant concessions till a final session at the end of March. This might start on a Monday and go on all week, with breaks for consultations or referrals to working parties; sometimes the President would have to keep the Council at work into the night of Friday to Saturday. Then at last, Ministers might be prepared to make the necessary concessions: on returning home they could defend their action by pointing out that they had struggled to the last. Sheer exhaustion also played a part. It was customary for a glass of whisky to be served at midnight, which may have had a mellowing effect; on the other hand, the unappetising "Council sandwiches" were a disincentive to prolonging the discomfort too long.

As matters became increasingly critical, the President would restrict more and more the numbers of advisors allowed to each delegation in the Council chamber. Ultimately, the Ministers might be left with just their top civil servant, or even no advisor at all, in the hope that they might be more willing to give way on a crucial point with no witnesses on their own side. This was a nightmare for the Secretariat, which also had to restrict its numbers, yet still had the responsibility of recording whatever was finally agreed. Sometimes we tried to hide some of our staff in the interpreters' cabins (the full complement of interpreters was still required), but the interpreters did not much like this. Another tactic was to get our technicians to wire up some extra headphones in a corridor behind the cabins, but this had to be done very discreetly.

There were occasions when, despite all this, the deadline for settlement was missed. Then a legal fiction was invented: "stopping the clock"; and the current market measures just continued a little longer. As personally I never witnessed this, I cannot say whether clocks in the Council chamber were actually stopped; if the delay became too great, the procedure could undoubtedly have faced a legal challenge, though to my knowledge, this never happened. When finally an agreement was reached, the resulting regulations published in the *Official Journal* bore a date at the end of March…

By 1973, the "market regulations" of the CAP were well established, but they required constant adjustments and therefore took up most of the time in meetings. Initially, my own main responsibility was "socio-structural" policy – measures aimed at consolidating scattered plots, helping small farmers to retire or retrain for other jobs, and assisting farmers with greater potential to enlarge their holdings. This had lagged behind: the Six had adopted the first measures only in 1972. Now the major issue was how to accommodate the three new Member States, bearing in mind that their farm structures were significantly different from those of the Six, and on the whole much better.

The Danes had a particular objection to a scheme for giving early retirement pensions to farmers: their farmers already benefited from their national pensions system and this measure would actually have put retiring farmers in a better position than people in other sectors. Up to this point, the Commission had generally sought uniform measures across the Community. This approach was justified in the early stages, when common policies had to be created and would have been undermined by too many exceptions; it was also appropriate for market regulations, where different levels of aid would cause distortion of competition. But with a wider range of Member States, and particularly where farm structures were concerned, a more flexible approach was called for.

There was a legal problem in that if farmers in Denmark, for example, were unable to claim benefits that were available to farmers in other countries, they might demand redress from the European Court of Justice. Eventually, the legal experts came up with a form of words to justify differentiating such aids where objective conditions were different, and this became the basis for more flexible "directives" – a form of legislation which gives more scope than "regulations" for Member States to imple-ment the measure in the way most appropriate to their circumstances.

This must have been one of the first cases where the Commission began to tone down its urge for uniformity. At one stage I found myself mediating between Danish experts and Commission officials, the latter being initially reluctant to compromise; in fact, it had not been their practice to consult too much with national officials, no doubt fearing pressures that would undermine their objectivity.[5] But as time went on, and with new officials joining the Commission, including those from new Member States, it modified its attitude. This was notably the case as regards standards for traded goods, including foodstuffs: such standards are clearly desirable to ensure fair competition and to help consumers to know what they are buying, but the Commission did become more discerning in deciding which standards were necessary and those which were not.

The CAP at this time was giving relatively little benefit to Italy; in fact, political instability had prevented Italy from playing a significant role in the establishment of the policy and its subsequent development. At last, Italy got a more effective Minister of Agriculture in the person of Giuseppe Marcora. Following an unsatisfactory (from his point of view) Council session, he gave a press conference back in Rome at which he denounced this situation and attributed it to the lack of an Italian in a significant Commission post. The French, he said, had the Director-General (Rabot), the British had the Deputy DG for markets (Franklin), Germany had the Deputy for socio-structural policy (Helmut von Verschuer), while Italy only had the Deputy for external relations (Pizzuti): i.e. said Marcora, nothing at all (*"un bel niente…"*). Result: von Verschuer and Pizzuti were switched around.

This was an unusually blatant case of interference in the staffing of a European institution, but in fact, as I myself had already learned, all appointments at the Director-General or Director level were controlled by national authorities, though usually more discreetly. In fact, most appointees subsequently respect the principle of impartiality. In this case, the Italian demands were justified, and soon afterwards the Commission produced a "Mediterranean package" with aids for irrigation, infrastructure improvement, afforestation and other items. This looked good on paper and no doubt was good for Marcora's political reputation: in fact, Italian administration being less than perfect, implementation lagged behind.

Other regionalised measures followed; the main beneficiary was Ireland (though for field drainage rather than irrigation). Later, with further enlargements of the European Community, Greece, Spain and Portugal were to benefit from "Integrated Mediterranean Programmes". Even though the funds were not always well used, this was an important policy development, enabling a transfer from the Community budget – hence, principally from the richer countries – to the poorer regions.

However, the switch in the Commission, from my point of view, was not an improvement. Von Verschuer was a competent and courteous man with whom it was easy to co-operate. Pizzuti was a Neapolitan whose French was difficult to understand; I also found him difficult to work with. He once tried to bully me into doing something I considered wrong; he was not my boss. But we did find ourselves in each other's company when, shortly after Greece's accession to the Community in 1981, their Agricultural Ministry invited Pizzuti and Raymond Craps from the Commission and myself from the Council Secretariat to make a study visit. This was a most interesting tour of different agricultural regions, by helicopter from Athens to northern Greece (we had a spectacular flight around the Meteora monastery). About the same time I was taking an interest in rural development in Crete and my Greek was serviceable, so I asked a lot of questions. This upset Pizzuti, who clearly felt that I was trespassing on Commission territory. There was of course no problem with my old friend Raymond Craps.[6]

The other issue of agricultural policy which occupied much of my time was "green money". This was such a complicated matter that even in the Commission only a few officials fully understood it, and it was rumoured that they were never all allowed to travel on the same plane at the same time. Their expert-in-chief was a German named Joachim Heine, for whom I had great respect and with whom I collaborated closely. On our Council Secretariat side, we were just two or three who could claim to have mastered this subject. (When I lectured on agricultural policy – see next chapter – I needed a whole academic hour to explain how this worked; in my *Government and Agriculture* book, this occupied five pages.)

Basically, the problem arose from trying to apply a system of common prices to countries with different currencies (this was long before the euro). The prices were fixed in an artificial unit of account, but if one country – say France – devalued its currency, that meant that the guaranteed price would become higher in francs: good for farmers, but liable to provoke inflation. If another country – say Germany – upvalued its currency, guaranteed farm prices there would fall, provoking farmer outrage.

So the Commission invented a very complex system of "green rates" (substituting for real exchange rates) and "monetary compensatory amounts" applied to trade in farm products between the Member States (subsidies on imports into a devaluing country, levies on imports into an upvaluing country). As one can imagine, this led to lengthy and intricate discussions.

It gave rise to the only case where I can lay claim to have modified Community policy. At an early stage, the Commission started sending proposals entitled "agro-monetary" regulations. "Not so", I said. "*Agro*" is a Greek root, fine in "agronomy", since *nomos* is Greek; but "monetary" comes from the Latin *moneta* (as does "culture", in "agriculture"), and requires the prefix "*agri*". And so it was from then on.

This linguistic matter calls to mind a little-known feature of the Council Secretariat's work: its "jurist-linguist" group. After the Council (in whatever formation) has agreed on a Commission proposal, this bunch of remarkably gifted people set to work to produce in all the official languages the texts which will be regarded as equally authentic and published in the *Official Journal*. To this effect, one of its number reads aloud the latest version of the text in its original language (formerly French, now more likely English) while the others check the translations in their respective languages (there were six in the Community of nine Member States). Normally the jurist-linguists manage very well, and the finalised texts can be formally adopted by the next Council session as an "A-point" (i.e. without discussion). But sometimes there is a doubt as to what the Council intended, and in such cases a member of the Secretariat who was present in the Council chamber may be called upon.

The most difficult problems arise when the texts on which the delegations agreed say different things: it is not unknown for a Council President, in desperation, to push through an agreement knowing full well that some countries have different interpretations. The Secretariat's worst nightmare is when such an issue cannot be resolved and must be referred back, probably to the SCA in the case of agricultural policy matters, otherwise to the COREPER.

Fisheries policy

The Treaty of Rome had not specifically provided for a common fisheries policy. But in 1970 – before the first enlargement of the Community – the Six had agreed that, in principle, their fishermen should have access to the waters of all other Member States. As part of the "acquis communautaire", the candidate countries had little choice but to accept this.

In 1976, fisheries became a major issue. Partly in response to Iceland's unilateral declaration of a 200-mile zone but also in line with international developments in the law of the sea, Community Member States extended their rights to marine resources from 12 to 200 nautical miles from their coasts. This gave Britain and Ireland the largest fishing areas, but to which under the previous agreement fishermen from other Community countries would have equal access.

So a new common policy was needed to manage fisheries in the expanded zone. Proposals started to arrive from the Commission, and the CFP was added to my remit in the Council Secretariat; in the following years, it was to take up at least as much of my time as agriculture. It was an area where the Secretariat sometimes had an unusually active role. The Commission took some time to get itself organised for this new task: at first, fisheries policy came under the Commissioner for agriculture and the Agricultural Directorate-General. In the Council Secretariat, my small but very competent team followed the negotiations from the start.

The first Commissioner responsible for fisheries, as well as agriculture, was the Dane, Finn Olav Gundelach. When a DG for fisheries was created, the first Director-General was an Irishman, Eamonn Gallagher. Both were extremely able men, and tough negotiators, which was necessary in a very conflictual area. Gundelach had been Executive Secretary of GATT (General Agreement on Tariffs and Trade) in Geneva, and had been one of Denmark's chief negotiators in its accession procedure. Gallagher had held senior positions in the Irish civil service.

They were totally contrasting personalities. Gundelach was intellectual, austere, and appeared physically weak – in Council sessions sometimes so haggard that one wondered if he would stay the course (he always did at that time, but he died of a heart attack while in Strasbourg for a meeting in 1981, aged only 55). Gallagher was robust, a *bon viveur*; fishing for salmon and trout on the Irish rivers was his favourite pastime. Both were highly competent in their different ways, but they detested each other. Once, while waiting for the start of a Fisheries Council in Luxembourg, I walked to the other end of the table for a word with Gundelach. Seeing Gallagher enter the room, Gundelach said: "There's my Director-General: he's drunk again!"; as I passed Gallagher on my way back he said: "You've been talking to my Commissioner: he's on drugs again...". Somehow I got on well with both of them, which was necessary.

When Greece joined the Community in 1981, the new post of Fisheries Commissioner was taken by Giorgios Kontogeorgis, one of the Greek accession negotiators. This suited Gallagher admirably, for Kontogeorgis was an amiable but ineffective man, and had no previous experience with fisheries. So Gallagher was in full control, and made this obvious even in Council sessions. In consultations outside the Council chamber, it was sometimes embarrassing to observe him side-lining his hierarchical chief.

Creating a fisheries policy raised two different but interconnected issues. One was to preserve stocks in the common 200-mile zone; the other, how to allocate this scarce resource. Already by the mid-1970s, several species in the North Sea and the North Atlantic were over-fished. The Commission proposed several elements – mostly based on existing national measures – which included minimum net sizes (so that the smaller fish could escape), and bans on fishing for particular species at certain periods (to permit breeding). But basically the system depended on quotas for each of the main species. These would be based on Total Allowable Catches (TACs), supposed to reflect the advice of independent experts. It was then necessary to decide how to divide up the available catch between the Member States, and how much – if any – to allow to third countries.

From the start, the policy was misconceived, and in the work of the Fisheries Council and its dependent bodies one could see this happening, as each country fought to defend its own fishermen. Even the supposedly scientifically-based TACs were questioned and often increased. The central issue was (and remains) the distribution of quotas. Inevitably – and this should have been obvious to the Commission – when an overall resource, already limited, has to be shared out between a number of countries, each will claim as much as it can and the end-result will be a figure higher than the total originally aimed at (the same happened with milk quotas under the CAP).

Fisheries quotas also suffer from the defect that in practice they can only be checked on landing. Although in principle inspections can take place at sea, it is impossible to prevent fishermen throwing overboard immature fish or fish of a species for which the quota is already exceeded – these fish are unlikely to survive.

Nevertheless, quotas were the mainstay of the Commission's proposals. I have always suspected that this suited Eamonn Gallagher rather well. As the quotas had to be renegotiated annually, it put him in a central position, negotiating with the competing countries both outside and inside the Council. Maybe he had in mind the similar role of the Commission under the CAP in the annual price-fixing exercise.

The long-term solution with fisheries, as with agriculture, would have been through socio-structural reform, in this case decommissioning fishing-boats and paying fishermen to retire or retrain for other jobs. Admittedly, this is difficult since many coastal towns are highly dependent on fisheries. But in any case, it was not a major plank in the Commission's approach, and was certainly unpopular with fishermen, hence with politicians. Nevertheless, during a German presidency in the second half of 1978, their Permanent Representative in Brussels, Walter Kittel, attempted to reinforce this part of the proposed policy; we worked on this together.[7] I think this was a personal initiative or at any rate one supported by the German Foreign Office (fisheries was not an overall German priority) but probably not by their Agriculture Ministry (also responsible for fisheries). In any case, it did not come to anything significant.

In fact, though as already said, the Secretariat was more actively involved in the fisheries negotiations than in agriculture, it is difficult to claim any success. One failure on my part had practical consequences. The first Commission proposals provided for the quotas to come into effect on 1 January and to be revised annually. I pointed out to the Commission that this would mean a difficult Fisheries Council session every year at the end of December, and that since there is no particular season for fisheries almost any other date in the calendar could be chosen. To no avail; and the result was as I predicted. Every December the Council has to meet, usually in the week before Christmas, in a session which often lasts right up to the vacation, causing major inconvenience to everyone concerned, particularly to delegates who have to travel long distances.

There was a further problem, which did not concern the Commission but did make life difficult for the Secretariat and no doubt for national administrations. When the Council has reached an agreement, it does not usually come into effect immediately: the Member States have to formally confirm their acceptance, taking into account whatever amendments have been made to the proposed regulations. With a Council concluding just before Christmas, and regulations due to enter into force on 1 January, one can easily imagine the difficulties. Confirmation was usually sent by telex. On one occasion, several confirmations were still outstanding on 31 December, and I was practically alone in my office in the Council building waiting for them to arrive – this was not a job that could be left to a secretary, in case something went wrong. Midnight was approaching and nothing was happening. So I went upstairs to the telex office and found it empty; moreover, I discovered that someone – perhaps the cleaners – had pulled the electric plug for the telex out of its socket... I pushed it back in, and the machine began to churn out the missing messages.

There was a more serious failure. In the latter half of 1980 the Presidency fell to Luxembourg – not noted for the importance of its fisheries, hence able to take genuinely objective stance. By this time the negotiations seemed well advanced and an overall agreement possible. The Luxembourg representatives came to us to say that they intended to make this a major aim of their presidency, and that since they were somewhat lacking in fishery experts they would rely on us for advice.

They were as good as their word, and all went well until the inevitable December Council. A package agreement was then close, but some further work on the quota distribution was required and was entrusted to a working party. Unfortunately, the Luxembourgers did not have anyone available to chair this meeting, and in such cases the custom was to pass the job to the Netherlands – next in the alphabetical order and another Benelux country.

But the Netherlands did have a major interest in fisheries, and the Dutch chairman (De Zeeuw, head of their Ministry and a powerful character) used his position to draft a report pulling some fish (sole, in very short supply) in the Dutch direction. What was worse was that he took this off the French quota, disregarding the fact that great efforts had been made to get the French on board. There was a discussion in the office of my Director-General in which I tried to stop this report going to the Council. But my Director-General – who had not followed the discussions so closely – was not prepared to confront De Zeeuw. The report went to the Council, the French hit the roof, and the opportunity was lost.

A comprehensive fisheries policy was only adopted in 1983. In the face of declining fish stocks, "reforms" were adopted in 1992 and 2002, with limited success. In May 2009 the Commission released a "Green Paper" on *Reform of the Common Fisheries Policy* (available on Internet), which has launched a new round of negotiations. The document stresses "the current reality of overfishing, fleet overcapacity, heavy subsidies, low economic resilience and decline in the volume of fish caught by European fishermen" and admits that "the current CFP has not worked well enough to prevent those problems". It observes that "all decisions are taken in Council at the highest political level" and that this has resulted "in a focus on short-term considerations at the expense of the longer-term environmental, economic and social sustainability of European fisheries".

One might say, especially with hindsight, that the CFP is in some respects more important in the long term than the CAP. The more the CAP conceded to farmers' pressure in terms of price support and protection in one form or another, the costlier the policy would be for the Community budget and the more consumers would have to pay for their food. There would also be environmental consequences – not much considered in the early stages – arising from intensive farming. But most of these effects would be reversible: the CAP has been substantially modified to take account of environmental concerns, and on the whole the land and wildlife can recover.

With the CFP, the environmental issue – depletion of fish stocks – was known from the start. Failure to devise an effective policy to conserve stocks could lead to the disappearance of some species in some regions. And that is what has nearly happened: in the North Sea, Irish Sea and West of Scotland, stocks of cod, haddock, herring, plaice and sole have fallen to levels from which in some cases they may never recover.

The European Parliament

In the initial years, members were appointed to the Parliament by the Member States from their own national parliaments. But the Treaty of Rome had specified that the European Parliament must be elected by universal suffrage using a common voting system. The first such direct elections were held only in 1979.

The powers of the Parliament were initially limited: it could only give the Council of Ministers its opinions on Commission proposals. Subsequently it got extra authority over the Community budget.

Members of the European Parliament were entitled to address questions to the Council of Ministers. In practice, it was the Secretariat which answered them. This was one of the most tedious tasks, for the questions were usually silly, submitted by an MEP only to boost his own sense of self-importance and – since questions and answers get published in the *Official Journal* – to create the impression that he was being active.

Presidents of the Council, in its various formations, had to appear from time to time before the Parliament. Again it was the Secretariat's task to prepare a speech. The main object was to say as little as possible while giving the impression that one was saying something important. I hated this task and found it rather difficult, but it was an art which some staff members – including my Director-General – had become good at.

On such occasions, the President would be accompanied to Strasbourg by a member of the Secretariat. Once only this fell to me (it was not a popular task). It was a Belgian presidency and the Minister of Agriculture was Antoine Humblet, a francophone Socialist (unusual, as this post was usually filled by a Flemish politician, appointed in practice by the very powerful Flemish farm lobby, the *Boerenbond*).

For the journey he commandeered a plane from the Belgian air force; approaching Strasbourg, we were told that we could not land there because of fog. Instead we landed on the German side of the Rhine at a Canadian NATO base, to be received by some rather bemused staff, who nevertheless quickly produced a French-speaking officer. He offered an official car and driver to take us to the European Parliament. However, since my previous visit, the Parliament had acquired a new building and I did not know where it was; neither, of course, did our Canadian driver. In fact, he dropped us off at a building with lots of European flags, which however turned out to be the city hall.

Consequently, we arrived late at the proper building, only to find that the debate for which the Minister was required had been postponed till the afternoon. No matter: M. Humblet proposed that we have lunch at a restaurant he had heard of, the *Crocodile*. This was the most expensive place in Strasbourg; the Minister, moreover, ordered some of the dearest items on the menu. Assuming that I had an expense allowance, he expected me to pay. In fact, I had no such allowance, but I could hardly tell him that. On return to Brussels I had difficult explanations to make before I could get reimbursement.

M. Humblet was a courteous man, and competent in his job. Nevertheless, such experiences left me with a low regard for politicians, of whatever party. Likewise, Secretariat staff generally had a poor opinion of the members of the European Parliament at the time. Though its opinion was formally required for most Council decisions, the Council in fact paid little or no attention to their content. Occasionally the Council reached a decision sooner than expected, and we would have to check quickly whether the Parliament's opinion had been received; no one was interested in what it said. There was nothing to prevent the Council doing the opposite of whatever the Parliament had recommended.

The Economic and Social Committee was held in even lower esteem. This institution had been created by the Treaty of Rome on the model of the similar French institution, to provide a forum where representatives of employers and workers could discuss Community policies and give their opinion on Commission proposals. It did sometimes produce worthwhile reports, to which perhaps the Commission paid some attention. But as these had no legal force, the Council ignored them. The least desirable post in the Council Secretariat was that for handling relations with the ESC. In the successive institutional reforms of the Community, the ESC has escaped notice, possibly because it is so insignificant: otherwise, money could be saved by abolishing it and no-one besides its members and staff would notice the difference.

The British "renegotiation"

The British general election of February 1974 was won by the Labour Party under Harold Wilson. Although the new government did not challenge the principle of British accession itself, Wilson had severely criticised the compromises accepted by Edward Heath. So the new Foreign Secretary, James Callaghan, in his initial address to the Council of Ministers on 1 April 1974, called for a fundamental renegotiation of these terms. Under pressure from opponents of accession within its own ranks, the government had to accept that the outcome would be submitted to referendum.

For Community staff in Brussels, the British call for "renegotiation" was received with consternation, and for recently-recruited British like myself, with embarrassment. It had already been difficult enough to fit in with the existing staff (more of this later); now it felt as though the carpet had been pulled from under our feet.

Volumes have been written about the issues involved in the "renegotiation" – I contributed some of this myself. That is not my purpose here. Suffice it to say food and agriculture issues were prominent, since in accepting the *acquis communautaire* the Heath government had also accepted the Common Agricultural Policy. The Wilson government now wanted longer transitional preferences for imports of New Zealand butter and Caribbean sugar.

More significantly, it wanted a reduction in the British contribution to the Community budget – a matter also related to agriculture, since the relatively high British contribution stemmed from the fact that Britain imported much of its food from outside the Community, upon which under the CAP import levies were charged to the benefit of the Community budget, while agriculture was a relatively small part of the British economy, meaning that Britain received proportionately less in CAP subsidies.

Consequently we awaited with trepidation the arrival of the new Minister of Agriculture, Fred Peart, for his first Agricultural Council session. He had been one of the most vociferous opponents of Britain's entry into the Community. Indeed, his initial speeches confirmed our fears. But soon something happened. I am persuaded that this began at the bar on the top floor of the Charlemagne building, next to the Council chamber, during a recess. Fred Peart was in fact a sociable character, and as a North Country man, he enjoyed his beer. So, as he discovered, did the German Minister, Josef Ertl, a Bavarian: so I found them enjoying a drink together and getting on rather well despite language difficulties. Peart had fought in the Second World War, which might explain his hostility to things European; he probably had limited peacetime experience with other nationalities.

Indeed, on another occasion – also at the bar – I overheard his conversation with my Italian Director-General, Luigi Fricchione. In a very short time – and despite the fact that Fricchione had limited English – he had discovered that during the 1944-45 Italian campaign they had been on opposing sides in the same battle, both in the artillery (it may have been Monte Cassino). This he treated as a great joke: "Boom boom" pointing one way, "Boom boom" pointing the other way...

So Fred Peart's anti-Europeanism quickly became much attenuated. (His successor, John Silkin, was much less amenable, always with an eye for the political advantage to be gained from any situation.[8]) Of course, the substantive issues remained. Yet it became apparent to us in Brussels that the "renegotiation" was to a large extent a sham. Harold Wilson had no intention of taking Britain out of the Community. He was saddled with the referendum, but being a particularly wily politician, he chose to fight on ground where there was a chance of getting adequate concessions.

Most of the other Community countries were equally anxious to keep Britain in, and were therefore disposed to make the face-saving concessions which Wilson needed. The French, unsurprisingly, were the main obstacle. Indeed, they refused to accept that such a thing as "renegotiation" could happen: in our reports, we had to find some kind of circumlocution (which is why the habit of putting the term in inverted commas has remained with me).

So by March 1975 a deal was approved, which above all introduced a "correction mechanism" for Britain's budgetary contribution. On this basis the Wilson Government recommended that the electorate should approve the results of the renegotiation. An intense campaign to influence public opinion then began. Opposition to the agreement came mainly from the left wing of the Labour Party; the Conservatives (including their new leader, Margaret Thatcher) were mostly in favour. Anyway, when the national referendum was held on 5 June 1975, continued membership of the European Community was approved by 67.2% of the voters, on a turn-out of 64.5%.

The budget issue continued to plague Britain's relations with the Community. In 1978 the Labour Government (now under James Callaghan, following Wilson's resignation) protested once again at the amount of the British contribution, which it believed to be still too high. And of course Margaret Thatcher, after coming to power in 1979, fought a further and tenacious battle over Britain's budget contribution.

At one point, this led to a British "empty chair". Mrs Thatcher was copying the tactics of President de Gaulle in 1965, when he set out to curb the authority of the Commission and especially to limit the scope for the Council to take decisions by majority vote, as the Treaty had provided. Then, for several months, no French delegates had participated in Community meetings, until the "Luxembourg compromise" was reached. This stated that where "very important interests" were at stake, the Council would endeavour to reach solutions which could be adopted by all members; in the French view, this meant that discussions must continue until unanimous agreement was reached. This brought a fundamental change in the nature of the Community, and set the stage for many arduous sessions of the Council. In fact, de Gaulle anticipated a development which would probably have happened in any case. Edward Heath, in his agreement with Pompidou on Britain's accession, happily endorsed the "Luxembourg compromise".

The British "empty chair" probably created more problems for themselves than for the others, who might even have been quite relieved not to have troublesome British delegates sitting at the table (France was indispensable to the Community, Britain was not). But it meant that the British could not keep in touch with what was happening. This led to the only time when my UK nationality became relevant. fisheries negotiations were on-going, and my Director-General actually proposed that I should brief the British Deputy Permanent Representative at the end of the current meetings, which I did. This was William Nicoll, with whom I had quite good relations. Eventually Margaret Thatcher got some further budgetary concession and British delegates took up their seats once again.

The budgetary issue provoked another, more significant development. At one point in 1982, while Mrs Thatcher was fighting her battle, the Agricultural Council was nearing agreement on its annual price-fixing exercise; in fact, the British had already subscribed to an informal agreement. However, at the last moment, the UK delegation was instructed to withhold formal agreement, with the intention that this would force through a satisfactory conclusion to the budget negotiations in another Council.

Hence, the Agriculture Minister (Peter Walker) invoked the "Luxembourg compromise" in an attempt to veto the prices agreement. To the astonishment of the British delegation, this tactic was refused by the President (Belgian), by the Commission and by all other delegations including the French. The "Luxembourg compromise", they said, required a "vital interest" in the matter in question and could not be used as a link with a different issue in another Council; moreover, the British had in fact already agreed to the prices package.

This became a major constitutional crisis. The British brought in their Ambassador, Sir Michael Butler. The Commission President also appeared to underline the significance of the event: this was Gaston Thorn – a Luxembourger, but his country had always opposed the "Luxembourg compromise" (so-called simply because that is where De Gaulle's "empty chair" was resolved). To the consternation of the British, the package was voted through with the agreement of all other delegations.

It so happened that I was sitting within earshot of the UK delegation so I overheard their discussions, which became quite frantic. It did not occur to these very high-level people that there was one way they could have blocked or at least delayed the vote: there was an item in the package which required unanimity – and in these cases the package stood or fell as a whole. I kept quiet…

The Council Secretariat

The Secretariat at that time was not a happy ship. On arriving from the OECD, where staff relations were generally good, I had some big adjustments to make. I think all of us from the three new Member States had such difficulties. For one thing, we found an existing staff which seemed to have lost whatever enthusiasm they might have started with: we were, on the whole, more European-minded than they were. Also, not unnaturally, they resented us occupying some senior posts. In my case, my service had previously been managed by a Belgian at the Head of Division level (A3); I came in above him as a Director (A2). He was very courteous about it, but after a while he got a transfer and I could not blame him.

A lot of the trouble came from the fact that the Secretariat is a small institution as compared with the Commission (my own "Directorate" had just a half-dozen professional staff), within which promotion prospects are inevitably limited. Nevertheless, most people regarded employment there as a career (OECD staff, on the other hand, come and go). And most of the staff, though very good at their secretariat job, have no special qualifications which might enable them to move to the Commission, for example, nor indeed to move to equally secure and well-paid jobs else-where. Indeed, movement even within the Secretariat was rare: if you started working on say, the market regulation for fruit and vegetables, there was a strong chance that you would continue working on that for years, maybe all your career, with just a couple of grades of promotion. This did not make for much job satisfaction. (A mobility programme has since been introduced.)

The legal staff are a special case: they have a big responsibility, since they have to pronounce, sometimes at short notice, on the legality of some decision which the Council is about to make. Though some of them were not easy to work with, I had a high regard for their expertise.

I had a particular problem on arrival in that the other Director in the Agriculture Directorate-General, a Frenchman, did all he could to profit from my inexperience of Council ways. He managed to get the first choice of newly-recruited staff; my haul included an unfortunate young Dane who could not work in French and he gave up within a year.

There was also the issue of seats at the meetings of the Special Committee for Agriculture and the Council. At OECD I was used to taking whatever seat near the chairman was available. Not so in the Charlemagne. The sitting-order was: our Director-General on the left of the chairman; then whichever Director was responsible for the item under discussion, then the other Director, then the representative of the Legal Service. (My first brush with the Legal Service was when I inadvertently took the chair reserved for them – nobody had bothered to warn me.) The two Directors were supposed to switch seats according to the item being discussed, only my colleague was always most reluctant to surrender his position. This did not greatly bother me, but my own staff said that I must insist, otherwise it would reflect badly on them too. A similar situation had arisen in my early days when I was allotted a room with two windows: no, said my staff, a Director must have three windows – which in due course I acquired.

These were examples of the prevailing formality and rigid hierarchy: the staff seemed to have acquired the worst bureaucratic methods of the Germans, French and Italians. In the OECD, "Anglo-Saxon" habits had led to a comparatively relaxed attitude: there, if I wanted to talk to one of my staff, I just walked down the corridor to his/her room. In the Charlemagne, if my Director-General, Fricchione, whose office was just across the corridor from mine, wanted to see me, he called his secretary to call my secretary to ask me to go to him... And if I was working in shirt-sleeves, I realised that he would be upset if I came into his office without my jacket. I also realised that some of my own staff were embarrassed if I dropped into their office without warning.

Fricchhione, to his credit, had not been parachuted into his position but had worked his way up (the post, of course, had an Italian label on it just as mine had been created with a British tag). I respected his long experience in the Secretariat, but our relations remained distant. He was used to the Secretariat's bureaucratic and hierarchical habits and I think he was baffled by my somewhat unorthodox ways.

In OECD, we had useful printed forms for sending notes to other staff, headed "From/ To/ Subject/ Date". In the Charlemagne my naïve request for such forms was greeted with bewilderment. Instead, one typed out *"Note à l'attention de Monsieur le Président"* or whatever other title was appropriate, and continued in the same pompous manner.

There was in fact a Secretariat style used for all notes and reports, with standard phrases, limited vocabulary, and it was best to stick with this to avoid misunderstanding. It was a stereotyped language which could lend itself to computerised translation: by the time I left, the Head of the English translation service was in fact making experiments in this direction.

Formality also affected the issue of how to address one's colleagues. This is a problem in all international contexts. OECD worked mainly in English, and was relatively easy-going: one could just use surnames, without a title, for the men at any rate. In the Council Secretariat it was different. In the first place, French was the working language, and this requires "Monsieur", "Madame" or "Mademoiselle". Moreover, it raises the problem of *vous* or *tu*: basically, you don't use the latter unless you have known someone a long time, and even then, to use it in a work context could suggest favouritism. The same applied to the use of first names: on the whole, one didn't.

These were minor irritants. More important, the staff was strongly unionised and strikes were not uncommon. These were usually led by the Council translators, who admittedly had very little job satisfaction, and often were required to work long hours translating urgent documents. Nevertheless, considering the high pay and the job security, I had little sympathy for action over pay-related issues, nor had several of my own staff. This could lead to friction: a Frenchman in my service – an admirable, hard-working colleague who always refused to join a strike – was once accused of being a *collaborateur*: that, with its allusion to events in Nazi-occupied France, was an insult which he resented deeply.

Interpreters for the meetings were provided by the Commission. Since many were free-lance and valued their jobs, they were less inclined to go on strike, but if they did, their action was extremely effective: without them, the Council, its committees and working-parties simply came to a halt. They too had a legitimate complaint in the tendency for meetings to drag on in the evenings, and here some satisfaction was obtained from which we all benefited.

I have already referred to the lack of career prospects for most of the staff. This was aggravated – in all the European institutions – by the practice of *parachutage*, whereby Member States appointed their own choices to the top jobs. As I have explained, my own appointment depended on the British, much to my annoyance, but at least the practice is more acceptable in connection with the accession of new Member States, when new jobs are created at all levels (as was the case with my post). At other times, it represents an opportunity lost for existing staff. It is also, of course, contrary to the spirit and the provisions of the Treaty.[9]

In 1973 one post at the Director-General level (A1), with responsibility for the Community budget, had been filled by a British appointee – Kenneth Christofas, who had participated in the entry negotiations. In 1982 he was due to retire, and there were several A2 candidates within the staff, among whom I was the longest-serving Briton. But the British authorities again nominated one of theirs – in fact, Bill Nicoll, whom I have already mentioned and with whom I had quite good personal relations.

It so happened that at about the same time, an opening had arisen at the A2 level, and a Luxembourger had been appointed from outside the staff. This had been contested by the inside candidates, including one of the legal staff, Bernhard Schloh – a most capable lawyer – and he had taken the case to the European Court of Justice. So – in consultation with Schloh – I threatened to do the same. The authorities were alarmed: we had the law on our side. They could only appoint outside candidates if no-one from within the staff could be considered capable of doing the job. As I had been dealing with the budget implications of the CAP (which as already mentioned took most of the budget expenditure) and had an economics background, they could hardly use this argument. If they lost both cases, the whole *parachutage* system would be blown open, and not just for the Council Secretariat but for all European institutions.

However, I had discovered a clause in the staff regulations – Article 50 – which provided, in the case of A1 and A2 posts, for retirement "in the interests of the service". This in fact was the counterpart to *parachutage*, enabling authorities to remove serving officials and replace them with national appointees. It had never been used in the Council Secretariat. Obviously, it entailed a financial loss; but I did my calculations and reckoned that the pension would meet my requirements. At what I judged the appropriate moment, I asked for an interview with the Secretary-General, Niels Ersbøll, and put this to him; I had also asked for the head of administration to be present, which was just as well, for Ersbøll had never heard of Article 50. Anyway, he jumped at it, and so it happened.

I am not sure what other staff thought of this: many certainly thought I was mad to give up a very lucrative position. Maybe it would have been better for them if I had pursued and won the legal battle. Schloh and others continued to fight their case and eventually won: the Luxembourger had to go. But Schloh, mostly unfairly, did not get the post: in fact, he stayed at the same level until he retired.

The A1 post went to Nicoll. But at the same time, the job was changed. Instead of Budget affairs, an important and interesting area, Bill Nicoll had to take over relations with the European Parliament, at that time one of the most boring tasks in the Council Secretariat. I was well out of it, and could even indulge in a little *Schadenfreude*. And at the age of fifty-one, I could hope for more interesting things ahead.

Looking back, I felt that I had achieved very little in my ten years in the Council Secretariat. There were a couple of cases, both in relation to fisheries, where I might perhaps have exerted a little influence on the outcome, but even that did not work out.

Most of those working in the "Brussels" context are small cogs in a very large machine. I think I did my job adequately, and perhaps handled reasonably well its most interesting feature, that of keeping on good terms with counterparts in the Commission and in the national delegations (knowledge of several languages helped here), and thus occasionally helping to work out compromises.

But my only indubitable contribution to Community policy remained that one letter, already mentioned: "agri-monetary" instead of "agro-monetary" policy...[10]

All those working on agricultural policy – Secretariat and national representatives – worked hard throughout the year; only August was free of meetings, barring emergencies. As already mentioned, the Special Committee for Agriculture (SCA) met every Monday and Tuesday to prepare for the sessions of the ministerial Council, except when that Council itself met which was roughly once a month. Working parties took place on the other days; so reports from a working party at the end of the week might have to be ready for the following Monday, and so on. Often the Secretariat would sit down immediately after a meeting, sometimes late in the day, to draft a report which would go to the translators next morning or even the same evening.

There was a compensation which I felt in the circumstances was fully justified. Under each six-month presidency, the SCA was invited to meet in the country of the chair. The meeting in fact was rather a formality, usually lasting just a day. Around this the host country arranged a number of visits – often but not necessarily connected to farming. I did not personally get on all these trips – it depended on having an agenda item for which one was responsible – but several of these jaunts were enjoyable, besides helping to develop personal contacts among the participants.

One which remains fixed in my mind was to the West of Ireland. We were based in Cork, and were offered a coach tour around the peninsula west of Killarney, during which we saw absolutely nothing but mist and the occasional glimpse of sea or mountainside. But there was a grand display of Irish step-dancing in the evening. In Denmark the meeting was once held in Aarhus, giving the opportunity of a tour to the northern point of Jutland where the Skagerrak meets the Kattegat. In a freezing wind, we (or some of us) dutifully took off our shoes and stood on the very point with one foot in each sea. We were revived by an excellent lunch with copious doses of *aquavit*; it was a very somnolent coach party on the way back to Aarhus.

The grandest venue in my experience was to Venice, where we were lodged in a hotel far more expensive than any I would normally used. There was an interesting visit to San Georgio Maggiore and its monastery, and a formal dinner at the Lido (which made me think of "Death in Venice").

It was also the practice for Germany (with its capital still in Bonn) to invite the SCA to the annual Green Week – the national agricultural show – held paradoxically in West Berlin. This was of course a matter of waving the flag in the still-divided city. Having no countryside to show, other topics had to be found. On one occasion there was a visit which I found particularly interesting: to the waste disposal factory. Having no hinterland to dump its rubbish, West Berlin had to find other solutions, and was well-advanced in the separation and recycling of its waste, years before most other places in the world became so environmentally-conscious.

---

[1] The Council now has a massive purpose-built edifice opposite the Commission's Berlaymont, with the tongue-twisting name "Justus Lipsius" after a 16th-century Flemish philologist and humanist. He is less well-known than his predecessor Erasmus, but a street of that name had been demolished to make way for the new building, and perhaps the list of famous and non-controversial Europeans was getting used up. The Berlaymont, incidentally, is named after a former convent on that site.

[2] There was a special reason for British insistence on getting this Commission post, though I only realised it later. The United Kingdom had developed an "Annual Review" of agricultural prices and costs, supposed to provide an objective basis for the annual fixing of guaranteed prices to farmers. The British had fussed a great deal about this in their entry negotiations: they had the idea that it would impose some restraint on tendencies to go on raising farm prices. And they wanted a British official in Brussels to oversee this process.

Their choice for the job, Peter Parkhouse, was not an economist himself: it was typical of the British civil service to think that a well-educated and cultured person would somehow be able to direct a team of trained economists. Unsurprisingly, this didn't work out, and after a few years he actually proposed to me that we switch jobs. This very sensible idea – he would have been much more suited to the Council Secretariat than I was – was however stymied by his number two, who probably thought I would be more difficult to manage.

Moreover, the British did not achieve their main aim. World prices of agricultural commodities rose sharply soon after British accession to the Community, so that application of the "objective method" would have led to substantial increases in guaranteed prices. Some complex manoeuvring became necessary to avoid this outcome.

3 One might think that for Germany too, as another highly industrialised country, the farming interest would be secondary. Not so, for complicated historical reasons which I set out in my *Government and Agriculture in Western Europe, 1880–1988.*

4 De Gaulle brought to the Presidency of France a *grandeur* of style which was largely maintained by Pompidou, Giscard d'Estaing and even Mitterrand. The dignity of the office has come down with a bump with Nicolas Sarkozy, whatever his other merits.

5 At the first meeting of the Special Committee for Agriculture which I attended, in June 1973, the Commission was represented by the Deputy Director-General Heringa (already mentioned in the previous chapter as one of the architects of the CAP's market regulations). I remember him as an authoritative character, laying down the law and basically telling the national delegations what to do. He was replaced by a British appointee, Michael Franklin, who was equally competent but at least managed to appear much more flexible.

6 This case study of Western Crete, along with another on Apulia in Italy, was published by the Arkleton Trust – *People and Policies in Rural Development* (1982). In carrying it out, I had the assistance of a former student at the College of Europe, Aphrodite Syngellaki. We had interesting discussions with farmers and with village mayors, often in some very remote areas.

7 Sessions of the Fisheries Council were prepared not by the Special Committee for Agriculture but by the Committee of Permanent Representatives (COREPER), chaired by the Permanent Representative from the presiding country. To be precise, there were two bodies: COREPER I attended by the Deputy Permanent Representatives and COREPER II in which the Ambassadors met. The essential work was done by COREPER I, which met at least once a week. During my time, the Ambassadors seemed mainly concerned with setting up the European University in Florence – a job which, knowing little about academic life, they botched quite badly – see next chapter.

8 John Silkin was adept at getting to the journalists – the British ones in particular – waiting on the ground floor of the Charlemagne building (the Council sessions took place on the top floor) just before the time they had to file their reports, thus giving them little chance of checking what he said with other delegations or, for that matter, the Council Secretariat. The official press conference took a little more time to organise.

Silkin also appeared to pay more attention to his political adviser than to his civil servants. In this he may have initiated a regrettable trend, recently denounced in a report by former "mandarins" entitled *Good Government,* which among other criticisms points to the sidelining of impartial civil servants in favour of "sofa government" by advisors whose loyalty is to party and not to the public interest (cf. http://www.bettergovernment-initiative.co.uk).

[9] For Commission staff, a further cause of grievance arises from the practice whereby Commissioners appoint a number of advisers to their cabinet (another import from French administration). These appointees bypass the very tough entrance examinations through which regular staff are recruited, and on the departure of the Commissioner in question, some demand to be integrated into the regular staff. Moreover, their allegiance is liable to be more towards the political and national priorities of their Commissioner.

This issue is reflected – unintentionally – in the book by Derk Jan Eppink, *Life of a European Mandarin: Inside the Commission* (2008). Eppink was in the cabinet of the Dutch commissioner, Frits Bolkestein. He seems to have spent a lot of his time fighting the senior Commission officials. In the 2009 elections for the European Parliament he gained a seat for a right-wing Flemish party, which has allied itself to the British Conservatives and other "euro-sceptic" and anti-federalist parties.

[10] In 2006 I was contacted by a professor from Strasbourg University, Michel Mangenot, in connection with a projected report on the Council Secretariat. The administration had arranged for him to meet former and current A1s and A2s. I suggested that he should also talk to the lower grades: what mattered most was the constant hard work by many competent junior officials who could never even hope to reach those levels.

I also found that Mangenot was under the impression that Niels Ersbøll, Secretary-General from 1980, had brought a new impetus to the staff. Not in my experience, I said. Soon after his arrival he held one meeting with his A1s and A2s and promised more, so that we would be kept informed of broad developments, but no further meetings were ever held.

Writing this, I have tried – unsuccessfully – to locate the projected report. I have however discovered – and read with some incredulity – Ersbøll's own assessment in www.ena.lu :

> "Compared to the Commission, career patterns are generally more stable and predictable in the Council Secretariat. I consider this to be a general advantage. To preserve its identity as an international body, and indeed its 'esprit de corps', which is crucial for its efficiency, it must remain free of national interference with recruitment except for a very small number of posts at the top, notably that of the Secretary

General. Even at the level of Director General, Member States ought to interfere as little as possible with the choice of candidate as long as the so-called national balance is preserved. Indeed, the best service Member States can render to the efficiency of the Secretariat is to accept that *qualifications should always precede other considerations including the 'national balance'."* (my italics).

VI. ACADEMIA

I had a foot in the academic world from quite an early stage in my career. After those couple of years in London working in Political and Economic Planning on the birth of the Common Agricultural Policy, and then in 1973 getting into the OECD's Agricultural Policies Division, it was clear that agricultural policy was to be my field.

It was also clear that agricultural policies left much to be desired, with their extensive market intervention, price support and protection. It was not difficult to criticise them from an economic angle, as indeed we did in OECD. But I felt that more explanation was needed, and I decided to embark on my own account on a study of the origins and evolution of these policies up to the formation of the Common Agricultural Policy.

For a couple of years I worked very hard in the evenings and on most Saturdays – Sundays remained taboo – collecting all the material I could find in the Paris libraries. This was not an easy task. The library of the *Faculté de droit* was one useful source; the *Bibliothèque nationale* was a last resort (its catalogue was confusing and it took ages to get a book out of the system). The most useful for my purpose was the *Bibliothèque de documentation internationale contemporaine*, as it possessed works from various European countries and was conveniently situated in the 16th arrondissement, not too far from the OECD; moreover, you were allowed to borrow up to five books at a time. There was, however, a problem, as I discovered once when I came to collect my quota which I had ordered the previous day: only three of them were available. The others, I was told, were "too heavy". Why did that matter? Because, it turned out, the stock was mostly kept somewhere on the other side of the city, and books ordered were collected once a day by one of the staff going in the metro with a suitcase … Some essential works could be ordered from abroad, and eventually I had gathered sufficient material, which formed an extensive bibliography in several languages.

The actual writing of the book was relatively quick. It was much easier then than it is now to find a publisher: Jonathan Cape in London took the book up, and was a pleasant firm to deal with. The work came out in 1964 under the title *Agriculture in Western Europe – Crisis and Adaptation since 1880*. It contained chapters of a general nature plus case studies of four contrasting countries: the United Kingdom, France, Germany and Denmark.

My thesis was simple. During the Great Depression of the late nine-teenth century, falling commodity prices on world markets had forced most European countries, especially France and Germany, into protectionist policies. The UK had held to free trade principles: many British farmers went out of business, but in due course a more efficient farm structure emerged. Denmark had the most constructive policy, taking advantage of low international grain prices to build up a highly competitive livestock and build up cooperative marketing. During the economic crisis of the 1930s, most countries went further, intervening directly on agricultural markets through government agencies: this was the case of France and especially of Nazi Germany. Even in the UK, Marketing Boards were set up in an attempt to raise returns to producers. During the Second World War, farmers were encouraged to raise their output through price supports in various forms. Continued support and protection after the war soon led to surpluses of wheat, milk and other products in France and other continental countries. Unwilling to raise barriers to imports from the Commonwealth or to raise food prices to consumers, Britain pursued a different method of support: "deficiency payments" to farmers to make up the difference between market prices and substantially higher guaranteed prices.

This, basically, was the situation when the EEC was setting up its common agricultural policy. The outcome mainly reflected systems in Germany, France and the Netherlands. An unsavoury and little-noticed fact was that the main instrument for protection consisted of variable import levies, which had originated as part of Nazi agricultural policy.

The book was well received in academic circles and became a reference work for agricultural policy courses. Naïvely, I imagined that the force of my arguments would influence government policies and lead to more rational policies: this of course was an illusion. Maybe some civil servants were aware of the book, but I doubt very much that it came to the notice of any Minister of Agriculture.

I produced two later editions, in 1982 and 1989, in each case updating the story to cover later developments in the CAP and to some extent in the USA and other countries; I also delved further back in time to give more attention to the origins of farm structures in feudal times and subsequent developments such as "enclosures" in Britain.

While in London with PEP, I had joined the Agricultural Economics Society (AES). At the time, this was a gentlemanly body which met in a comfortable hotel in Harrogate. It included some quite grand names in the agricultural economics field, and I found it rather intimidating. Gradually the Society changed. The Harrogate venue was expensive, and the conferences began to be organised on a university campus, during academic vacations so with accommodation in student rooms. Some of these campuses – I remember Exeter and Aberdeen in particular – were very pleasant.

While in Paris, I also joined the *Société française d'économie rurale* (SFER). This operated differently: its conferences were always held in Paris, participants had to find their own accommodation and there was hardly any of the socialising which was a pleasant aspect of the AES. However, I found its debates interesting. The differences in the names was significant: *"économie rurale"* suggests a broader approach than that of just agricultural economics.

Since the British and French governments were constantly at loggerheads over agricultural policy, I found it disturbing that the academic professions were likewise divided, with the British constantly stressing considerations of efficiency and profitability, the French more concerned with social and rural aspects. A clear illustration of this arose when the introduction of milk quotas was mooted. British experts were opposed: quotas would bring inefficiency in the allocation of resources, and prevent the market doing its job through price adjustment. Quite true. But the French tended to be in favour, because they saw that quotas would help to maintain dairying activity in difficult areas such as the Massif Central, and that seemed a legitimate aim even though production costs would be higher.

Milk quotas were in fact introduced under the CAP in 1984, disregarding objectors who predicted that they would be very difficult to remove (there were precedents in the US with tobacco quotas). Indeed, as I write now, the Commission wants to remove milk quotas, but farmers are protesting because – as with fisheries – quotas have preserved surplus capacity, keeping in business farmers who otherwise would have been forced out.

Having my contacts – and sympathies – on both sides, I later took the initiative in organising a joint Anglo-French seminar. Language was obviously a problem, and there was no budget for professional inter-pretation, but it did prove possible to find enough competent people on both sides with enough knowledge of the other languages to make a meeting possible. The first such event took place in 1984 at the Centre for European Agricultural Studies under Wye College in Kent. It went well, and was followed by a return match the next year at an agricultural institute near Versailles. I am not sure whether these events led to a significant meeting of minds, but at least the alternative points of view were better understood.

Being an official in OECD did not significantly restrict my academic freedom – in fact the activities were complementary and OECD was usually quite happy to finance my travel for such purposes. Thus I was able to give talks in various places and contribute articles to professional journals, including both the *Agricultural Economics Review* of the AES and *Economie rurale* of the SFER.

In due course I was put on the committee of the Agricultural Economics Society (which enabled me to push the Anglo-French project. Then, as it is the custom of the AES to elect a new President each year, I got my turn in 1984/85. The President is expected to give an address, in which I claimed to be the first "European" President of the Society since unlike my predecessors I had spent almost all my career outside the UK. My topic was the growth of overproduction under the CAP and the sort of policy adjustments needed – in particular replacing price supports by direct aids (something which happened several years later). There was nothing very original in this, but I did innovate to some extent at least in the context of AES debates – by asking whether intensification and specialisation had not gone too far, and whether "low input-output" systems, using less fertiliser, pesticides, etc., might not deserves closer consideration. Critique of the "productivist" farming model was already well under way in France and I could cite interesting developments in other continental countries.

I followed this up by inviting as guest speaker to the following conference (a presidential privilege) the chief scientist in the Ministry of Agriculture, Frank Raymond, who had been working along these lines. He gave a talk which I thought interesting and original, but some of the younger members of the Society found this all too provocative and criticised him for his "bad economics". That was probably true but missed the main point; of course, the concept of reducing farming intensity has gained extra appeal as concerns over the rural environment have increased.

The agricultural economics profession, like economics in general, has changed over the years, becoming increasing mathematical, to the extent that for me – and perhaps for others of my generation – many articles in a review such as the *Journal of Agricultural Economics* became unintelligible. The reverse of this is that my own approach, based more on historical and "structural" analysis, probably has less appeal to the younger generation.

Consequently, I appreciated all the more being elected at the time of my retirement in 2000 to the *Académie d'Agriculture de France* – a purely honorific position in an ancient and prestigious institution, but which demonstrated that former French colleagues had not forgotten my efforts in earlier years.

Though it was unusual for Council Secretariat staff in Brussels to engage in outside activities, during my ten years in that post (1973-83) there was no serious objection to my giving the odd talk or writing the occasional paper, provided this did not conflict with my duties nor give away any confidential information. In fact, being able to explain how the Council functions and sometimes to give an up-to-date account of an ongoing negotiation was probably useful.

The most stimulating venue during this period was the College of Europe in Bruges (founded in 1948, so it predated the European Community) which at that time provided a one-year diploma course to students from all over Europe. They were usually selected by their national administrations and came with a government grant. Consequently the standards and the degree of previous knowledge varied, but on the whole the level was high. Both Spain and Portugal consistently sent each year a relatively large number of extremely competent youngsters: these countries were already preparing for entry into the European Community and had seen the utility of a College of Europe training. Greece also sent a substantial number, who tended to be either very good or rather bad. The United Kingdom did not seem to attach much importance to the College and sent relatively few. While Western Europeans (and Greeks) were in the majority, there were occasional students from the still-communist countries of central-eastern Europe. Once there was a young Chinese (from Communist China) who mysteriously found his own way to the College: he became one of the best students I ever had.

The College operated in French and English, and all candidates were supposed at least to understand both languages. The College had three "dominants" of which economics was one. There were no permanent teaching staff: lecturers came from other institutions, usually just for the day. I owed my appointment to my old friend Geoffrey Denton, with whom I had worked at PEP in London. By this time he was a professor at Reading University; he was also head of economics at the College of Europe. Incredibly – in view of the significance of the Common Agricultural Policy – there had previously been no course on agricultural policy, so this became my task. This turned out to be a popular choice among students, who were well aware of its relevance.

So for six or seven years, on Saturday mornings, I travelled from Brussels to Bruges by train, usually preparing my presentation on the way. Though I had given occasional lectures quite often, this was the first time I was responsible for an entire course. I did not start too well: I still had in mind the Cambridge tradition of elegant *ex-cathedra* lectures. However, I soon realised that something much more flexible was needed:

these were (mostly) mature students, and we benefited mutually from questions and discussion.

There was plenty of material. I have already pointed out that it could take several sessions to explain the complicated "agri-monetary" rules, for example. And these were serious students, many of whom were looking to a career in national administration or maybe the Commission: they were not afraid of detail. More significant, however, was what I could tell them about the Council decision-making process, since that was something they could not get from textbooks nor even from most other lecturers.

As I have pointed out, agricultural policy at the time turned around the annual "price-fixing" negotiations, starting with Commission proposals in January and due to end before the onset of the milk marketing year on 1 April. This fitted conveniently with the academic timetable: by January my students had a good grounding, so I was able to tell them week by week what was going on (the specialised press had most of this anyway, so I was not stretching the rules of confidentiality too far). Travelling back from one of these sessions, I had an idea: instead of explaining all this, why not let the students find out for themselves? So we started to prepare a "simulation" of the Council negotiation. Role-playing exercises have since become quite common, but here we had an unusual opportunity to enact in real time an on-going process, on the basis of the actual Commission proposals.

There were enough students to allot two or three to each country, plus at least three to the Commission. No-one was allowed to represent their own country. In the preparatory phase, the students were to find out as much as possible about the real position of the country, using news reports, and I also encouraged them to make contact with the national representations in Brussels – several of whom proved quite co-operative. The role of President I kept to myself, which enabled me to ensure that the proceedings followed Council practice (and, I admit, enabled me to work off a great deal of frustration).

The real Council had three months to work on the Commission proposals: we conducted our negotiation over one weekend in March, just before the final Council session. It proved a fascinating and instructive exercise. The start could be sticky, as some students had difficulty playing themselves into their role. One I remember telling me he could not possibly defend the position of the country to which he was allotted because it was so contrary to the economic principles he had been taught: after an hour or so, he and others had forgotten those principles as well as their own nationality. I particularly remember a young Greek lady vigorously defending the French position, with which she would certainly have disagreed in other circumstances.

Over the half-dozen occasions on which I conducted this simulation, we never reached agreement. But we did identify the major issues and stumbling-blocks, sometimes before the real Council had got that far. Eventually this came to the notice of the representations in Brussels – one delegate even came as an observer – and after our event I would be asked what was the result.

The international composition and linguistic ability of the Bruges student body greatly facilitated this simulation. However, I did introduce it to the teaching at Wye College, and on one occasion at an agricultural college in Copenhagen, in each case with reasonable success.

The contact with students was the most positive aspect of the College of Europe. This was not just in the teaching context. For the students, meeting and working with youngsters from different backgrounds was in itself a great experience. And they had a lot of fun. National groups vied with each other in giving parties based on their respective traditions, to which I was often invited. And many of the students became my friends for years afterwards.

Quite a few did get jobs in the Commission, several in the Agriculture Directorate-General, and this sometimes proved useful when I needed to get some information or action quickly. There was one occasion – I anticipate on my next chapter – when I was organising a visit to Brussels by a group of Hungarian agricultural economists. This was before the collapse of the Communist regime, and I got a message from a former student to say that her boss in the Commission information service was about to veto the project on the grounds that all those "Commies" were not welcome. I was able to go to higher authority and the visit went through, very successfully.

Regrettably, relations with the Rector of the time were problematic. This was Jerszy Lukaszewski: I saw him as a dour Polish bureaucrat who took little interest in the teaching.[1] At a certain point he apparently wanted to remove Geoffrey Denton, and to that effect introduced a rule according to which heads of "dominant" must come at least once a week to the College. Geoffrey, having his other commitments, came every second week, but stayed two or three days. Anyway, he was evicted. I resigned in sympathy; other teaching staff expressed support but would not take effective action. The student body, on the other hand, in a gesture which I much appreciated, made both Geoffrey and me honorary members of the student association…

Wye College, in the village of that name in Kent, was at the time of which I am writing formally part of London University (it has since merged with

Imperial College). It was however about an hour by train from central London, an attractive village in delightful countryside. Suitable enough for an agricultural college, but disconcerting for overseas students – many from Africa – who arrived unforewarned at a tiny rural railway station.

The College had a reputable economics department, chaired for many years by Denis Britton whom I have already mentioned as having been my mentor in my first job in Geneva. I had had occasional contacts with the College and had lectured there from time to time. In 1984 Denis was due to retire, and the College did not have enough funds to make a permanent appointment. So for a year I filled the post as a Visiting Professor. In fact, I spent most of that academic year in residence – it was a very pleasant place to be – and ran several lecture courses.

The Principal said to me at the outset that my role would be to get the students more interested in "Europe". This was actually no problem: most of them saw their future in farming or in some related activity and were well aware of the importance of the Common Agricultural Policy. As already mentioned, I put into practice at Wye the "simulation" exercise I had developed at the College of Europe: not having such a mix of nationalities, this was not so easy but still worthwhile. And when I gave an open lecture on the CAP, almost the whole student body turned up (but few of the staff); indeed, this became an annual event for several years subsequently. If there was a problem, it lay rather with the staff, who were rather set in their ways. There were honourable exceptions, in particular John Medland who worked closely with me on my courses, including the "simulation", and later shared with me the responsibility for a seminar for Turkish officials organised by the Centre for Mediterranean Agronomic Studies in Montpellier. Sadly, a couple of years later he was killed in a motor-cycling accident – ironically, in Turkey.

In due course the College found the money to appoint a permanent Chair, for which I considered applying. In the end I decided not to do so: this was mainly because I could foresee trouble if I tried to get the staff of the economics department to work together in a coherent teaching programme, as would have been in the interests of the students. From OECD days I was used to working with a team: at Wye, most of the staff had their individual priorities and would have regarded this as interference. This seems to be a characteristic of universities: staff tend to lecture on the basis of the research topic in which they are personally interested. Anyway, the College made an excellent appointment in the person of Alan Buckwell, with whom I later co-operated in various ways.

Just before my year at Wye, the long-standing Principal, Dunstan Skilbeck, had retired. However, I already knew him, and frequently went to visit him at his home in a nearby village. Conversations with him were always stimulating – much more so than with most of the staff. He always wanted to know what I had been telling the students, and I would end practically repeating my latest lecture. It was an object lesson in how to retain a lively mind in old age. I last saw him in the village square, sitting very erect on his horse in full riding gear and about to go off with the local hunt.

I referred in the previous chapter to the efforts of the Ambassadors in Brussels to set up a European University Institute in Florence. This had been decided upon in 1972 by the original six EEC Member States but received its first research students only in 1976. Its stated aim is "to provide advanced academic training for doctoral students and to promote research in history, economics, law and the social and political and social sciences".

My own experience with this was limited but unsatisfactory. One of my College of Europe students went there, but for some time she was writing to me for advice on her research. I realised that there was no-one on the teaching staff to give her guidance. In fact, this seemed to be a general problem: the Institute was offering "training" in far too wide a field in relation to its staff resources. It has since improved very considerably.[2]

I also had some involvement with the European Institute of Public Administration in Maastricht. This was promoted by the Dutch government and set up in 1981. The Netherlands wanted some kind of European academic institution, but the post-graduate field was already largely occupied by the College of Europe in Bruges and the European University Institute in Florence. As a fall-back, the idea was to have an institute which would help to train civil servants in European affairs.

This did not quite work as planned: most EEC Member States had their own training arrangements for civil servants and did not see much need to send them to Maastricht. I was asked to run a number of seminars on the Common Agricultural Policy: almost all of these were attended by young officials from non-EEC countries (one group was from Vietnam, another from South America). With some other staff, I also participated in seminars organised by the EIPA in Macedonia and in Montenegro (both, of course, still part of Yugoslavia): interest was minimal and we got hardly any participants. Maastricht is a pleasant town, but after a while I felt that this work was lacking in purpose.

There is an International Association of Agricultural Economists, which holds large conferences every three years in different parts of the world. In 1976 the venue was Nairobi, where I gave a paper on "The decision-making process in the European Community with reference to agricultural policy", but I remember this occasion more for the subsequent safari through the national parks of Kenya and Tanzania than for anything in the proceedings. These events were, to my taste, too big and the proceedings too diffuse.

More to the point, a European Association of Agricultural Economists (EAAE) was established in 1975 in Uppsala (Sweden); I had participated in a preliminary meeting in Siena. This too held tri-annual conferences (in different years from the international body) and I attended most of these.

During my period at the College of Europe in Bruges, I had organised – with the help of the very efficient assistant in the economics department, Ivan Hodac – a conference on "Prospects for Agriculture in the European Economic Community" (the papers were published under this title in 1979). I was able to get the participation of the Commissioner for Agriculture at the time, Finn Gundelach (already mentioned), the Belgian Minister of Agriculture and a number of leading academics from various countries, so this was quite successful.

One of the contributors was Michel Petit, whom I have already mentioned: professor of agricultural economics at Dijon and then President of the EAAE. He asked me to prepare the forthcoming conference, on rural development issues, in 1981. This was an interesting challenge, particularly as regards the still-communist countries of Central/Eastern Europe whom we were anxious to involve – especially as this event was to be held in Belgrade.

When the association had been set up at a meeting in Uppsala, Sweden, some founder members wanted it to be Western but the majority decided that to ensure participation from Eastern Europe, the post of Vice-President should go to a Russian. The only Russian candidate was Viktor Nazarenko, whose academic qualifications were doubtful but who obviously had the support of his government; he used it to squeeze out any independent participation from the USSR or indeed from anywhere in the Soviet bloc. Such conference papers as we got in 1975 and 1978 – mostly from Nazarenko himself – were useless, mere propaganda vaunting Soviet technological progress (and ignoring the growing queues for food in Russian cities).

For the Belgrade conference we had valuable support from the Yugoslav member of the EAAE committee, Dusan Tomic, who contacted numerous institutions in the USSR and the other countries of the region; we also laid down strict procedures, setting dates by which proposals had to be submitted and subsequent dates for papers to be sent in, well before the conference. We were pleasantly surprised by the number of offers we received, and we accepted most of them. Alas, by the appointed time, none of those promised papers from Soviet-zone countries arrived. It was only after we got to Belgrade for the conference that Nazarenko turned up, bringing a few papers, for most of which he himself was once again author or co-author…

We had a tense committee meeting, with Nazarenko present, when in my role as programme secretary I refused to accept these papers as our rules had not been observed. I had support from Michel Petit, but other committee members took the view – bearing in mind the original decision in Uppsala but still naïve in my opinion – that we should make an exception in order to keep the Russians on board. "Which Russians?", I asked, to no avail.

However, after the Belgrade conference, the principle of rotation was applied and a Pole became Vice-President in place of Nazarenko.

In striking contrast to the intellectual stranglehold still exercised by Soviet authority, I recall that the Smithsonian Institution organised in Washington in 1976, to mark the bicentenary of the United States, a conference on "The United States in the World". The special feature of this event was that non-Americans were invited to give the papers, Americans only to comment. (I was asked to speak on agriculture, and my theme was "U.S. agricultural potential and its impact on the rest of the world in the past 100 years".)

I can think of no other country that would have had the confidence and the open-mindedness to adopt such a procedure.[3]

---

[1] Professor Michel Petit, who was appointed by the Rector to succeed me in the College of Europe post and has commented usefully on this chapter, remarks that he formed a more favourable opinion of Lukaszewski : besides ensuring the necessary finance for the College, he had a strong appreciation of its multi-national role in further education.

[2] The student in question was Susan Senior (now Senior-Nello), already mentioned in my Preface, who obtained a doctorate at the European University Institute and has settled in Italy. She has commented:

"What you said of the EUI was true then, but certainly not now. It has grown in numbers and resources and is now considered one of the best places in Europe to do a PhD. Various professors have Nobel prizes or the equivalent for Political Science. I have been constantly involved in research projects, summer schools, conferences etc. and find it a very stimulating environment."

[3] This seems the place to put together references to some of my writings which I hope have been useful – some are mentioned in other chapters.

The first edition of my main book (1964) was called *Agriculture in Western Europe – Crisis and Adaptation since 1880*. It had a French edition – *L'Etat et l'agriculture en Europe occidentale – Crises et réponses au cours d'un siècle*; there was also a Japanese translation. There was a second edition in 1981, then a third in 1989 under the title *Government and Agriculture in Western Europe, 1880-1988*.

In 1991 I produced *Farmers and Politics in France*: in this I translated and edited papers by five well-known French agricultural economists and political scientists (Arkleton Trust, 1991).

In 1993 I published *Food and Agriculture in a Market Economy – an introduction to theory, practice and policy* under my own imprint, "Agricultural Policy Studies", It was translated into Russian, Estonian, Latvian, Lithuanian, Polish, Czech, Hungarian and Croat.

Under this APS imprint I also published *Agricultural Policy in the European Union and other market economies* (2nd edn. 1997). I also edited and published studies mainly written by others: *Renationalisation of the Common Agricultural Policy* (1994); *East-West European Agricultural Trade* (1994); *CAP Reform: The Southern Products* (1997).

VII. THE COLLAPSE OF COMMUNISM
Moscow and St. Petersburg

In the course of 1989, Communist regimes collapsed in Poland, Hungary, Czechoslovakia, Bulgaria and Romania. The "Berlin Wall" was opened and a year later Germany was reunified. The Soviet Union made no attempt to intervene in any of these events. At the end of 1991 the Soviet Union itself collapsed, its constituent republics becoming sovereign States.

Since the beginning of the Cold War, we had formed the bad habit of referring to "Europe" when we meant "Western Europe", or even the European Community. The "Iron Curtain" had effectively cut geographical Europe in two: across the divide, contact was limited. Countries in the Soviet bloc called themselves "democracies", but communist parties ruled and permitted no real opposition. All major decisions were taken in Moscow, though this did not prevent dictatorships by national party chiefs. The media were strictly controlled. Dissidents were liable to denunciation and arrest by secret police.

The inhabitants had little opportunity to travel to the West, while visa procedures controlled travel in the other direction. There was in any case not much incentive to visit these countries. My own experiences were limited, but on occasions when I was in West Berlin I made a daytime excursion into the Soviet-controlled eastern sector. It was never a pleasant experience. Arriving at "Check-point Charlie", one was observed through binoculars by an armed guard on a watch-tower on the eastern side of the barrier; one's passport disappeared for inspection behind a screen. Taking the S-Bahn to the Friedrichstrasse station in the eastern sector – the only other option – was not much better. (One line of the U-Bahn passed under the eastern sector, where the trains rushed through empty, unlit stations.)

East Berlin looked grey and dismal. Even in the once-prestigious museum area, wartime damage was still unrepaired. At a time when West Berlin had become a thriving, active city, full of life and light, the eastern side and its people seemed miserable, making mockery of the communist claim that the Wall was there to protect the people from capitalist influences.

Despite the obvious and growing gap in living standards between eastern and western Europe, few people expected the communist regimes to crumble quite so quickly in 1989. The Hungarian rising in 1956 and the "Prague spring" of 1968 had been crushed by Warsaw Pact forces under Soviet command. But opposition had not disappeared, as became evident particularly in Poland where the "Solidarity" movement became too powerful for the authorities to suppress. And under Mikhail Gorbachev, the Soviet Union was no longer disposed to intervene with military force to support unpopular regimes (though this could not be counted upon at the time).

One can argue about what was the most important factor. Probably the whole edifice of communist rule had become so shaky that if any prop anywhere was removed, it was bound to collapse. In Poland in June 1989, the political process set in motion by "Solidarity" led to elections in which the Communist party lost its hold on power.

Meanwhile in Hungary important reforms were under way within the Communist party itself, and there had been a start in demolishing the fence on its Austrian border. On 19 August a "picnic" on the frontier was planned by the democratic opposition in Hungary together with Western organisations; it was understood that a small border post would be opened up for a few hours and for a limited number of participants. In fact, the news had got around and the officer in charge of the post was confronted by a large crowd seeking to pass through on foot. He decided that his instructions – probably left deliberately vague by the authorities in Budapest – did not require his small force to open fire, so he let them through. As the news spread, hundreds of families from East Germany who were camping by Lake Balaton, less than an hour's drive away, rushed in their Trabants and Wartburgs to get through. Via Austria, most of them reached West Germany, sometimes to stay with relatives not far from their starting-point in the east. This was an exciting moment in European history, captured on television as events unfolded. Shortly afterwards, Hungary officially opened its border. (See Annex I for a fuller account of these events.)

In East Germany itself, demonstrations followed in the major cities, particularly in Leipzig where on 9 October a huge crowd was allowed to demonstrate peacefully – with the slogan "we are the people". Then, on 9 November 1989, after a confused official statement, East German border guards allowed crowds to pass to West Berlin through the Brandenburg gate, and soon the Berlin Wall was demolished. The government of the "German Democratic Republic" lost all credibility; German reunification followed a year later.

In Czechoslovakia, the communist regime collapsed in December 1989 and the dissident playwright Vaclav Havel was elected President.

These were countries where the existence of opposition movements was known. More surprising was the sudden end of two ruthless dictatorships. In Bulgaria, the communist leader Zhivkov was evicted in November 1989. And in Romania, in December, Ceausescu and his wife were chased out of Bucharest, captured and summarily executed; this revolution claimed some 1,400 victims.

All these events meant that these countries of Central Europe and the Balkans were at last able to renew contacts with the West, and in particular to start forging closer relationships with the European Union. For me personally, this led to an active and fruitful involvement in the region during the 1990s, about which I shall have more to say in the following chapter. For the moment, however, I turn to events in the former Soviet Union.

In August 1991, Communist hardliners in Moscow attempted to seize power while Mikhail Gorbachev, President of the USSR, was holidaying at his dacha in the Crimea. The plot failed, largely due to the opposition of Boris Yeltsin, President of Russia. But Gorbachev's power was severely weakened. In December, Yeltsin took Russia out of the Soviet Union, which thereby collapsed, Belarus, Ukraine, Moldova, Georgia and the Asian republics becoming independent states.

The three Baltic countries – Estonia, Latvia and Lithuania – regained their pre-war independence.

Apart from my unpleasant tussle with Viktor Nazarenko in the context of the European Association of Agricultural Economists (see previous chapter), I had had no professional involvement in the Soviet Union. So when in September 1991 I received a call from the European Commission asking me to join an urgent mission to Moscow, my first response was that I knew little of the country and even less about its agriculture.

The reason for the call was that President Gorbachev had made an appeal to the European Community and to the United States for a very large amount of food aid. His policies of *glasnost* (openness) and *perestroika* (restructuring) had done much to loosen up the country, above all permitting freer speech, but his attempts at economic reform were half-hearted: the apparatus of state control was breaking down but market mechanisms were not yet permitted to function properly. This had led in particular to worsening food shortages, evidenced by longer queues and frustrated would-be buyers.

Hence the urgent request for food aid; and the Commission rightly wanted to send a small team to investigate the situation and find out what was really needed. The Commission had a small unit handling relations with the USSR, but an agricultural economist was needed.

Even in this situation, getting a visa quickly from the Soviet embassy in Brussels was still a traumatic experience; however, in late September I took an Aeroflot flight to Moscow with the rest of the team. Moscow then seemed a strange city. There were still barbed-wire barricades around the "White House" – the Russian parliament building, hence Yeltsin's headquarters – erected during the attempted August coup. Some of the persons we met had stood with him on that tank when he defied the conspirators; generally the atmosphere was tense.

We stayed in the prestigious *Metropol* hotel, opposite the *Bolshoi* – in fact there was not much choice. It was outrageously expensive: this was the only occasion when I hit the limit on my credit card, within a week. Getting a meal after a day's work was a constant problem: the *Metropol* had a rather grand restaurant, where a full dinner was the only option, and in the city there were a number of expensive night-clubs also offering dinners but not much else. It was easier to get champagne (Russian) or vodka than any other drink. We were saved by the new Pizza Hut, where in the dollar-only section one could get a place and a meal quickly. (A MacDonald's appeared about this time, much to the delight of Muscovites.)

The mission proved difficult. Officials in the Ministry of Agriculture seemed reluctant to provide the information we wanted, or perhaps just did not have any. In fact, the main usefulness of our mission was that our mere arrival had caused Gorbachev to reduce his demand substantially, which suggested that the original request never had much objective basis anyway. Perhaps I was more successful than the rest of the team, thanks to Inessa Frantseva, whom I had met at a seminar in Hungary: I had made it a condition of my participation that she would be my assistant and interpreter. She worked in an economics institute, gave valuable advice and put me in touch with a number of helpful experts.

Our head of mission decided that the team should go also to Minsk, Kiev and Almaty (Belarus, Ukraine and and Kazakhstan being of course still within the Soviet Union at the time). However, we were still waiting for an appointment with the Soviet Minister of Agriculture in Moscow. The Commission representative in Moscow, Michael Emerson, knew me (we had both moved from OECD in 1983, and I think he had been responsible for my inclusion in the team): he told me to stay in Moscow whatever happened, and said that in the absence of our head of mission I had full authority.

At this point a message finally arrived saying that the Minister was now ready to receive us. So with Inessa and just one young Commission official, I went along to the Ministry. We sat on one side of a very large table, confronting the Minister and his top official. The Minister – I forget his name, and soon afterwards he disappeared from public view – was an *apparatchik* of the old Bolshevik style; the head of the ministry was equally dour. The Minister tried to intimidate me, saying that he expected to deal with more important persons than me (in which he was right, but I had my authority from Michael Emerson). He took offence at my requests for information, saying that they had already supplied all necessary data and demanding to know why did I not just accept their requests then and there... Altogether, not a satisfactory interview, and while I had nothing to lose, I admired very much the courage of Inessa: it was still by no means safe for a Soviet citizen to face up to a Minister as she did.

Our mission returned to Brussels and made our report. One main point was that the food shortage was not so much due to lack of output – there was a lot of grain piled up and rotting in inadequate storage – as to inefficient distribution. Under a system of price control and state management, there was not enough incentive to produce and market efficiently. The western countries did subsequently provide some food aid but not to the extent that Gorbachev had requested. We were particularly concerned as to how any such food would be distributed.

Personally, I learnt a lot from this mission about the living conditions in Moscow at the time. Once while I was with Inessa in her institute, the monthly official food parcels arrived – this was the practice in institutions, factories etc. – and she took me to the office where these were being distributed. The parcels contained a few basic foodstuffs – flour, sugar, margarine, etc. – and such was the shortage in the shops that they were eagerly awaited. Inessa told me afterwards that some of her colleagues had said she should not have let a foreigner see this: they were ashamed, but she insisted that it was important that I should know about it.

I had seen the queues for food outside the *Gastronom* stores (an absurd name), and I knew that getting supplies for a family took so much time that people had to take hours off work to go shopping – unless they had a retired grandparent to do the job. So I said to Inessa that I wanted to spend a day in the same way as a typical Muscovite would have to do. With some reluctance, she agreed. We stood in long queues of tired, sad-looking people in dismal shops, without knowing what – if anything – would be available once we got to the front. A different experience was visiting an open-air food market: here there were fruit and vegetables in plenty, at a price. Some of this was brought by the sellers themselves, coming by plane from the south of the country, perhaps from Georgia or Azerbaijan. Such were the absurdities of the Soviet pricing system that the revenue from selling a few baskets of produce in Moscow would more than cover the cost of the air fare...

It was not long before a second request came to me from the Commission. This time it was to represent them in a World Bank agricultural mission to the USSR, which had recently been admitted to the Bank's membership. This turned out to be a large mission of nearly thirty participants, including some World Bank staff and others gathered at short notice from all round the world. Most of the latter had no experience at all of Russia. Neither had I a couple of months previously, but most of these persons did not seem bothered: they were "experts" in their respective fields, mainly technical. The purpose of the mission, not very clearly defined, was ostensibly to offer advice: I felt that in fact it was mainly to boost the World Bank's image in the country.

We were housed this time in the *Aerostar* hotel, between the city and the airport. This was (is?) a joint venture with a Canadian enterprise, as appeared from the fresh Arctic lobster flown in specially. Our mission had official cars and drivers; I preferred the metro – there was a station just across the road and the Moscow metro is an experience in itself. Each of the Bank team had been issued with a laptop computer, and a room in the hotel was taken over as a communication centre where they appeared to work busily.

But the mission was much too large, and ill-timed. It began in November 1991 and was planned to continue into the New Year. The Soviet Union was collapsing – on the tourist stalls of the *Arbat* the head of Yeltsin was replacing that of Gorbachev on the *matrouschka* dolls – and officials did not know from one day to another what would happen to them; spending time with self-invited foreign experts was not high on their list of priorities. I did rather better: once again I had enlisted the help of Inessa Frantseva, and much of the time I pursued my own programme.

We did all have a meeting at the White House (the Russian parliament building) with the Russian (not the Soviet) Minister of Agriculture. This was Alexander Rutskoi: formerly an air force officer, it was he who in August that year had flown to the Crimea to extricate Mikhail Gorbachev. He was also Vice-President of Russia under Yeltsin. Initially, he impressed us with his energy. He spoke of his plans to reform Russian agriculture. He had a pet project (which reflected his military background): the engines and compartments of obsolete submarines could be converted into dairies… He arranged for us to visit a pilot project and insisted that we return to him to give our views. This was an interesting visit – the dairy did indeed look like the interior of a submarine. But we were not convinced of the merits of the scheme, so the second interview did not go well, and as he did not seem to have many other ideas we were less impressed. (In 1993, Rutskoi turned against Yeltsin, becoming one of those who then occupied the White House until driven out by shelling by pro-government forces, with considerable loss of life; he was imprisoned for a while but like the other rebels was amnestied in 1994.)

Another field tour took us to a large co-operative, and several of our team took a particular interest in the machinery. We were shown a combine-harvester which, our hosts said, was not working well. it was getting clogged with grain. One of our experts poked around inside its works and came up with a technical explanation. I thought there was an economic explanation: the drivers were being paid for the job – i.e. harvesting a field – and therefore had no interest in maximising the output, rather in speeding up the machine beyond its optimal capacity and then getting home as soon as possible. Pay them by the hour, or even better by the quantity of grain collected per hectare, and the problem would probably disappear.

There was a much more serious issue. The World Bank economists on the mission were concentrating their efforts on constructing a computer model to predict the consequence of freeing the prices for foodstuffs. Price liberalisation was of course a general theme in World Bank policy, and there was little doubt that officially-determined pricing was a major cause of the inefficiency of Russian (or Soviet) agriculture.

However, I raised, first, a technical objection. To predict the effects of price increases on supply and demand, you need data on the effects of former price changes: in a controlled economy, it would be difficult to get meaningful results. No matter, they said, we can assume these relationships (price "elasticities") from experience in other countries: a doubtful proposition, in my view.

More significantly, I claimed that the exercise was pointless: given the gravity of the food shortages, it was obvious that liberalisation would cause dramatic increases in food prices. Whether they doubled or tripled or quadrupled was almost indifferent: in any case there would be devastating consequences. That was the policy issue which we should address, and I recommended that our advice should be to defer liberalisation until some kind of social welfare net could be introduced – maybe similar to the U.S. "food stamp" programme under which low-income families get vouchers entitling them to purchase specified amounts of basic foodstuffs. I had checked this with my Russian contacts, who thought that such a scheme could be introduced quite quickly.

I had no success with this argument: the Bank staff were set on recommending price liberalisation as soon as possible.[1] It has to be said that the same advice was coming from other Western economists at the time. In particular, Jeffrey Sachs, professor at Harvard, had advocated such "shock therapy" in Poland with some success and was advising the

Russian Minister of Economics, Yegor Gaidar, along the same lines. But I remain convinced that Russia was not ready for this treatment.

Indeed, in January 1992, food prices were liberalised, and the consequences have been described by Professor Robert Skidelsky:

"Within a day food prices rose by 250 per cent. But the queues – bane of the Soviet system - vanished overnight. It took time for the supply response to come through, and in that first year the Russians suffered terribly, their living standards dropping by as much as 50 per cent. They kept going only by taking to their plots of land and growing their own food".[2]

It is tempting to speculate. What if I had managed to persuade that World Bank team to leave their computer models and work on the basic policy issue? What if we had recommended deferring price liberalisation until there was protection for low-income families, and what if this approach had been accepted by the Russian side? The fact is that none of this happened, and apart from the immediate consequences, the whole concept of the market economy got a bad name in Russia, from which it has never recovered.

For my part, I withdrew from that mission and reported back to the Commission (which of course had neither the power nor the inclination to do anything).

This experience left me very frustrated, and I resolved to take no part in any other missions of this kind. At the same time, I could not forget all the admirable people I had met in Russia, who despite living under despotic rule had maintained their courage and integrity, and were still facing difficult challenges. I went to my favourite place in the Swiss Alps (Kandersteg), and after a week's reflection decided to do what was within my ability: to write a book in response to their needs. I came back with the outline already clear in my mind and wrote the book fairly quickly. I also decided to publish it myself (imprint "Agricultural Policy Studies"), so that I could set a relatively low price for sales in the Central/Eastern European countries (book prices there were extremely low).

The work appeared in early 1993 under the title *Food and Agriculture in a Market Economy – an introduction to theory, practice and policy*. In explaining economic theory, I laid some stress on qualifications to the basic principles of market economics, essentially deriving from "welfare economics".[3] The "policy" element was of course mainly but not exclusively the Common Agricultural Policy of the European Union: it was necessary to explain that this did *not* correspond to the criteria of economic efficiency. The final chapter discussed implications for transition from socialised agriculture and dealt with prices, markets and trade, farm structures and tenure, and "agribusiness". I dedicated this book to "all those men and women who despite decades of oppression under totalitarian regimes have had the courage to preserve their intellectual integrity".

The book was printed by a small enterprise in Prague, and I handled orders myself. It was successful though not quite in the way I had planned: not many copies were sold in the CEECs but on the other hand there was considerable demand for translations. As a result it was published in eight languages of the region. The translations were mostly done by academic staff and their universities published the work. I believe it was used extensively in university courses and also in Ministries of Agriculture. By this time, there was of course much more interest in the subject, particularly among the countries preparing for accession to the European Union.

This led to many interesting contacts, particularly as regards the Russian edition. This was begun by a young researcher in the Agricultural Economics Institute in Kiev (whom I met during a conference there) but was soon taken over by the newly-founded *Ekonomicheskaya Shkola* in St. Petersburg.

This institute had set itself the challenging task of introducing western economic thinking into the Russian education system. It had embarked on a series of publications in Russian of western economic texts, and my book on agricultural economics and policy fitted well into their plans. They worked on it very seriously and in some respects had to innovate linguistically, as some economic terms did not yet exist in Russian. This was particularly the case with the word "marginal", which in neo-classical economics has the precise and important meaning of the last unit of supply or demand, but in Russian it had no exact equivalent: they used the word *predyelny* which normally refers to a limit or maximum. They cooperated closely with me, querying anything that seemed unclear or incorrect: as a result the Russian version (an attractive hardcover publication) was better than my English original. It also helped to improve subsequent translations.[4]

On one point they were firm: the title. No-one, they said, wanted to hear about the "market economy", after their recent experiences of price liberalisation and privatisation. So it was called "Food and agriculture in economically developed countries" (*Syelskoe khoziaistvo i prodovolstvie v ekonomike razvitikh stran*)...

This collaboration led me to visit St. Petersburg several times, and as the staff of the institute were consulting me on several matters I became for a while a member of their advisory board. I greatly admired their enthusiasm, unleashed after all the years of enforced communist doctrine. In fact, I had to try to restrain some of their more ambitious plans.

St. Petersburg, like Moscow a couple of years earlier, still had limited tourist facilities but was of course a fascinating city. I was lodged in university accommodation, basic but considerably better than what the students had, and it was well situated on one of the beautiful canals in the centre. I had opportunities to hear wonderful concerts and opera performances.

Those early 1990s, in Russia as in the other Central/Eastern European countries, were a period of great change and great hope.[5] People no longer lived in fear; their living standards were still low by comparison with the West but they could look forward to improvements. Those countries which have been able to join the EU have on the whole improved their lot significantly – I discuss this in the following chapter. Among the others, sadly, not all those hopes have been fulfilled, least of all in the country which remains dominant, Russia.

---

[1] The report of that World Bank mission to the USSR and Russia, published later in 1992, did recommend some kind of food safety net, so perhaps someone had second thoughts. But this was of course far too late. The report itself pointed out that in the month after liberalisation (January 1992), retail food prices for major food items in urban areas rose to 5-7 times their levels of December 1991.

[2] This quotation is from Robert Skidelsky, *The World after Communism*, 1995, p. 152. A study published in the medical journal *Lancet* in January 2009 associated a sharp rise in death rates in Russia and other Central/Eastern European countries with economic "shock therapy". This referred more to the privatisation policies which in Russia followed price liberalisation, and which likewise were badly handled. The authors wrote that "Great caution should be taken when macroeconomic policies seek radically to overhaul the economy without considering potential effects on the population's health."

[3] Alfred Pigou's *Economics of Welfare* was one of the few works on economic theory which I enjoyed during my time studying economics at Cambridge (he had himself held the chair there in the early twentieth century). His main contribution – qualifying the general principle of market equilibrium – was to observe that where the activities of an enterprise have negative external effects, not reflected in its own accounting, there is a case for an offsetting tax; in the reverse case a subsidy may be justified. This is highly relevant to our current problems of pollution: it is curious that though numerous

Internet sources discuss (and sometimes criticise) "Pigovian" taxes and subsidies, there is hardly any information there about Pigou himself.

[4] Around this time I set about improving my Russian (in Geneva at the UN I had followed a basic course). This included an intensive week-long residential course near Brussels, organised by a formidable Russian lady – we thought she must have had KGB connections, but she was certainly efficient. The course was attended by many professional translators and interpreters. Besides the language sessions – which were tough, especially those dealing with Russian verbs – we could learn Russian songs and dances.

I became able to deliver a lecture in Russian if it was first written out for me, and once read a Chekhov play (*Uncle Vanya*) before seeing it on stage in Moscow. It is challenging to learn and I have subsequently forgotten most of it, but it is a beautiful language; at the time it was useful in all the Slavic countries though now a generation has grown up which prefers English.

[5] In 1992 the American philosopher Francis Fukuyama published his book *The End of History and the Last Man*. Someone has said that you need to be a very distinguished scholar to write anything quite so silly. The phrase actually comes from Hegel and a French-Russian philosopher of the mid-twentieth century, Alexandre Kojève, and it might make sense only in terms of a particular definition of history as "a single, coherent, evolutionary process, when taking into account the experience of all peoples in all times" (p. xii). Fukuyama's book is a lengthy discourse on the idea that the collapse of Communist regimes signified the end of that process, with "liberal democracy" becoming the only universally-accepted political regime; by "liberal" he apparently means freedom from official coercion but sometimes it seems equivalent to "capitalist".

Of course, for Russia and the other countries of Central/Eastern Europe, the collapse of communist regimes has certainly not meant the end of their history.

VIII. EUROPE (MORE) UNITED
Central/Eastern Europe

Already by December 1989, the European Union had adopted the PHARE programme of economic assistance to Poland and Hungary.[1] This was later extended to Estonia, Latvia, Lithuania, the Czech Republic, Slovakia, Slovenia, Romania and Bulgaria, and Association Agreements, which included reciprocal trade concessions, were established with each of these countries from 1994 on.

After throwing off their communist regimes and breaking free from the Soviet Union, the Central and Eastern European countries (abbreviation "CEECs")[2] were faced with a huge task of political, institutional and economic adjustment. They looked to the West for help, and particularly to the European Union.

The rural sector posed important problems. In most of these countries, farming had been collectivised according to the Soviet model. Some of those big units – State farms, collectives, co-operatives – worked reasonably well (more so perhaps than their Russian counterparts). But generally the system was inefficient and unpopular: a return to privately-owned farms was demanded. In some countries, this was hampered by a lack of data on previous ownership. And generally, the new farmers lacked experience and above all capital. Likewise, the socialised food marketing structures were inefficient and needed to be privatised.

In Poland, a small-farm structure had been kept. This raised other problems: holdings were mostly too small to provide an adequate living for a family; farm buildings were inadequate; modern equipment was lacking. This was not very different from problems previously encountered in many regions in the European Union. The solution had to involve rural development to provide jobs for the surplus farm labour.

When accession to the EU came on the agenda, a host of other problems arose. Under the Common Agricultural Policy, prices for farm products were maintained at levels far higher than those in the CEECs. Substantial price increases for CEEC farmers on accession would no doubt please them, but would push up consumer prices and probably provoke inflation, besides creating unjustified income disparities between farmers and other people. Moreover, the cost of supporting farm prices in the new Member States would add greatly to the already high cost of the CAP. So there was a problem also for the EU, which intensified pressures for reform of the policy.

My own involvement in the region had already begun in 1987 at a meeting of agricultural economists in the Food and Agriculture Organization in Rome. One of the participants was Professor Csaba Csaki, whom I had met on previous occasions: he was one of the few academics from the CEECs who participated actively in seminars and conferences outside the region, including conferences of the European Association of Agricultural Economists. At this time, he was Rector of the Karl Marx University of Economics in Budapest. I happened to ask him if he could consider inviting me there to give some lectures: to my surprise, he immediately agreed.

So before long I went to Budapest; this was at my own expense, as there was no fund to pay for the journey, but once there I was treated with great hospitality, being lodged in comfortable university quarters and frequently invited for meals. Budapest then seemed a gloomy place, particularly after dark when street lighting was inadequate; many buildings seemed badly in need of restoration. There was not much traffic, and I saw for the first time a strange small car – this of course was the "Trabant" from East Germany, flimsy but at least cheap. There were very few tourists, and not much choice of restaurants. Nevertheless, I grew to like Budapest, and to appreciate very much the courtesy and hospitality of the Hungarians, both on the personal level and in due course when seminars on various aspects of rural policy began to be organised in their country; such occasions never passed with an elegant buffet reception. Maybe this has something to do with having been part of the Austro-Hungarian Empire.

An initial problem for my lectures was the absence of an overhead projector, which I was accustomed to use; but the students were attentive and language did not seem to be much of a problem, although they probably had never had lectures in English before. Besides those I gave in the "Karl Marx" University (this later became just the "Budapest University of Economics"), arrangements were made for me to speak in several other universities and agricultural colleges. My subject was, mainly, the EU's Common Agricultural Policy. At that time, neither students nor most of the staff nor knew much about this and its relevance was not yet so obvious; nevertheless, there was strong interest.

On this and subsequent visits, I came to know most of the prominent agricultural economists in the country. An important consequence was that in 1988 I was able to organise a visit to Belgium for a dozen of these colleagues. Their Agriculture Ministry paid for their travel, and for their stay I obtained some financial support from the European Commission. I have already mentioned that at one stage this was nearly cancelled by the head of the agricultural information services who said that they did not want "all these Commies"... Of course, those Hungarian academics could not be so described: the country had already moved far along the road to democracy. On one occasion in 1988, as I was leaving the university on foot, Professor Csaki (who was in principle a member of the Communist Party) offered me a lift: he was going, he said, to a crucial meeting of the Central Committee and he hoped he would not be arrested. In fact, this turned out to be one of the occasions when further steps were taken to liberalise the system; the fact that reform came largely from within the establishment helped to make the Hungarian transition peaceful and successful.

In fact, the visit of the Hungarian agricultural economists to Brussels was very successful: most of the participants had never been to the west before, certainly not for professional purposes. They had useful talks with Commission officials, who were impressed by their interest and commitment. I also arranged for them to visit a food supermarket, whose manager explained to them its buying and selling methods. I believe that all this proved valuable to them after Hungary established a democratic regime in 1989 and later when the country prepared for membership of the European Union.

Central/Eastern Europe occupied most of my time and energy during the 1990s. The Association Agreements aimed at establishing a free trade area between the countries concerned and the EU, but for agricultural products full liberalisation was not considered possible so special arrangements were made, involving reciprocal reductions in import duties and, on the EU side, in the import levies it imposed on agricultural products.

This led to a complex pattern of concessions, and I asked experts from the countries concerned plus one from the Commission to contribute papers on the subject. Although we had no budget for this work, we managed to hold a very useful and enjoyable seminar together in a Hungarian village, thanks mainly to the efforts of our Hungarian participant, Judith Kiss from the Institute of World Economics in Budapest. I published the papers in 1994 under my "Agricultural Policy Studies" imprint (*East-West European Agricultural Trade – The Impact of Association Agreements*). This publication probably helped to make the authors better known in Western Europe.

There was a growing need in the CEECs for a better knowledge of EU policies in general, agricultural policy in particular. Here I was in a favourable position: I had my academic background in agricultural economics and I also had my experience in the Council Secretariat with the EU's political decision-making process. So I found myself being asked to give lectures or training seminars in various universities and in ministries of agriculture.

In particular, under the PHARE programme, "Policy Analysis Units" had been set up in several ministries of agriculture. These were badly needed: most of the staff carried over from their previous regimes would have been unable to rise to the challenge; apart from anything else, being brought up under the Soviet-oriented system, they knew Russian but usually no western language.

I had contacts with these new units in Warsaw, Bucharest and Sofia. They were staffed by competent, dynamic young people. Women pre-dominated, probably because on the whole women seem better at languages.[3] They were paid salaries topped up by PHARE to levels well above those received by regular officials.

While I was on a mission in Sofia (part of a contract by the Commission for an evaluation of PHARE activities) and getting valuable help from the PAU team, the Commission announced that these privileges would be withdrawn. The higher pay had of course caused resentment among other Ministry staff; nevertheless it seemed to me and to my colleague on this mission to be justified, as the expertise of these people was badly needed and without the top-up they would be lost to the expanding private sector, or to jobs abroad. We sent an urgent letter to the Commission recommending that this move be postponed, but I don't think this was heeded.

In the early 1990s, this work in Central/Eastern Europe gave me much satisfaction. As a former EU official receiving a pension, I could not be paid fees under PHARE or any other EU programme, as was right and proper. Sometimes I even paid my own travel expenses. But my contributions were appreciated, and my hosts responded as best they could, providing accommodation, arranging local travel and sometimes a small fee in local currency.

As time went on, however, the availability of high fees for consultants under PHARE or other EU-financed programmes attracted numerous "experts". In some cases they knew little about the countries they were supposed to be advising. This, I felt, devalued the activity; indeed I found that some of the officials I was dealing with assumed that I was getting these fees and that I was therefore at their beck-and-call. On what became my last visit, to Estonia, the head of the Ministry of Agriculture was asking me to correct translations for him during my visit, which I did not think was my job.

Moreover, as these countries began negotiating their entry to the EU, I was simply getting too much work: I could have been travelling almost every week to one country or another. And my own brand of expertise involved keeping closely in touch with what was happening in Brussels: there were constantly new documents to study, and I tried to maintain my contacts in the Commission, all of which took time. So I decided on my second retirement; 1 January 2000 seemed a suitable date, when I would be 68. And this time, I managed to forget all about agricultural policy...

My involvement in Central/Eastern Europe was not all hard work. I have already observed that working on rural issues has the advantage of bringing opportunities for interesting visits. One I remember in particular was in Ukraine, when following a conference in Kiev a small group of participants was offered a tour of the famous "black earth" area. This was very soon after the Soviet Union had collapsed and Ukraine was trying to find its feet in its new independent status. Agriculture in the Ukraine had undergone brutal collectivisation under Stalin in the 1930s; now, what should have been a fertile, prosperous farming region was struggling with the legacy. We visited a newly privatised farm, carved out of one of the former huge co-operatives: I greatly admired the courage of the farmer and his family in setting up a new enterprise with little management experience and where capital was badly needed for modern buildings and machinery. I had similar experiences in Russia.

At the other extreme, in Poland I was taken to visit a typical small dairy farm. The cows were kept all winter in a single shed, where straw was added daily to the manure and the cows were milked on the spot. The milk was left out in churns by the roadside for collection. Such farms, besides being unviable in modern conditions, would not even pass EU hygiene requirements.

In Romania, after a week conducting a seminar on the CAP in the Ministry of Agriculture,[4] I was taken on a weekend tour to the west of the country by a Belgian businessmen and his Romanian wife, Angelica Stoican, a well-known singer whose reputation clearly was very helpful to his contact-making. I saw a lot of the country, as far as the Western Carpathian mountains and the Danube, but I had mixed feelings about this trip. The businessman, who had some kind of import-export enterprise, thought – wrongly – that I could get some favour for him from the Commission. And I discovered along the route that he had given in advance a totally misleading impression of my position and influence in Brussels. In Craiova, the home-town of the sculptor Brancusi, I was treated to a special tour of the town museum on a day when it should have been closed; presented with some special memorial coins bearing reproductions of Brancusi's best-known works; and then taken by the city mayor to their principal winery – very interesting and the wine was good, but they obviously hoped I could do something to facilitate their exports to the EU and it was embarrassing to have to explain that I had no such power.

The attractions of Central/Eastern Europe were not just rural. With frequent visits, I grew attached to Budapest, especially as I saw it change from drabness to become a bright modern city and as the Trabants disappeared to be replaced by western cars; even Mercedes made their appearance. It is in fact two cities, separated by the Danube, dominated by Buda castle and the cathedral on the western bank; the Parliament building stands opposite. In my view, only Paris makes equally good use of its river. There are fine museums and art galleries. I discovered with pleasure the paintings of Mihály Munkácsy, and was particularly moved by the ancient crown of Hungary's first king, St. Stephen.

Prague is also a fine city, but I did not get to know it so well. At the time it was just beginning to attract substantial numbers of tourists. I particularly enjoyed the street musicians – actually, highly-qualified professionals earning some badly-needed extra money. In both Budapest and Prague, concerts and above all the opera were major attractions for me: seats were cheap relatively to opera houses in Brussels or Paris and easily available. Maybe the quality of performances was not so high, but in Budapest I heard an excellent production of Richard Strauss' *Rosenkavalier*, one of my favourite operas.

At this time – around 1990 – I was going through a Kodaly phase: a choir in which I was involved in Belgium had got rather stuck into a traditional repertoire and I was conspiring with the conductor to intro-duce new pieces. One of my professional contacts in Budapest sang in a good choir and took me to a rehearsal. Kodaly's choral music is superb: a difficulty is that most of it is in Hungarian and one needs to know how it is pronounced (translations rarely work because the accent in Hungarian normally falls on the first syllable of each word and that determines the rhythm). I did not learn much Hungarian – it is one of the most difficult European languages – but I did get to know the pronunciation well enough to guide our choir when I was back home. (We did perform some

Kodaly pieces in concert: while about half the choir liked them, the other half did not, so this was not a great success.)

Budapest and Prague were fortunate in escaping Stalinist architectural monstrosities. Not so Warsaw: the awful "Palace of Culture and Science" (237 m. high) is visible from all over the city. After destruction during the German invasion in 1939 and especially after the Warsaw Rising in 1944, most of the ancient city disappeared. But the Old Town has been magnificently restored; in the Market Square, even the stairs in the Historical Museum appear to have been worn down over the ages. Likewise the meticulous restoration of the Royal Castle; among its exhibits, Canaletto's paintings of Warsaw are particularly interesting. Probably it is this experience which has produced so much Polish talent in restoration work; I know a small Belgian château which has been entirely and beautifully restored by Polish craftsmen.

In 1990 I had the opportunity to visit Krakow. It happened to be the Polish national day (3 May) and I was in the royal cathedral in the castle precincts for the celebratory mass. The cathedral was packed, and the Polish national anthem was sung, with great fervour: this was the first time the people had been free to sing it for many years.

Bucharest too has its monstrosity, Ceausescu's megalomaniac "People's Palace". At the time I saw it, it was empty, and its future was being debated (it has since been put to use for ministries and for exhibitions). An entire area of the old town had been destroyed to make room for the palace; broad avenues and featureless apartment blocks were created. I stayed in one of these apartments, and was kept awake by the barking of stray dogs: these, I was told, had been made homeless when their owners were evicted.

I have fewer memories of Sofia, but perhaps I did not stay there long enough or did not have enough time after work to visit the city properly. Nearby, I did enjoy the famous "Valley of Roses". On a quite different occasion – I had gone with a Belgian group to learn Bulgarian folk dances – I spent a week based in Kyustendil. This is described as an "ancient" city, but then it was poor and depressed. It has an art gallery, but many of its works were not on display. However, the lady director of the gallery realised my interest in Byzantine art, and in a few days herself produced a beautiful copy of an icon – St. George and the Dragon – which now hangs over my desk; her fee was absurdly small and I gladly paid her more than she asked. Bulgarian dances, incidentally, are intricate, often involving irregular rhythms (such as five or seven beats in the bar); Bulgarians love dancing, and in a restaurant with a few musicians playing, people will get up and join in a circle dance with people they have never met.

I have already mentioned Moscow and St. Petersburg. Moscow I always found intimidating: it gave me a feeling of insecurity – irrational perhaps – as if at any moment the city could somehow swallow me up. The Kremlin must of course be visited for its splendid churches, but the name of the place conjured up too many sinister associations for me to feel comfortable. And there were too many unfortunate people sitting in the streets trying to sell a few used household items – even the toys of children who had presumably grown up.

My friend and ally Inessa lived in a suburb to the north of the city: to get there involved a long metro ride – not in itself a hardship, for the metro is one of the best things about Moscow – then a walk past depressing apartment blocks. The flat where she herself lived with her husband and their son was distinctly up-market by comparison, but the rooms were tiny. All the cars outside were parked in little individual garages of corrugated iron to protect them from theft or vandalism; that was the sort of thing which made me feel insecure. And there was the constant problem of finding somewhere to eat at a reasonably price. My best memory is of the Russian paintings in the Tretyakov gallery. It is now more than ten years since I was last in Moscow; I know it has changed immensely, I hope for the better.

Moscow is definitely a Russian city. Peter the Great created his city to look westwards, and so it does; with its canals and graceful buildings it is sometimes called the Venice of the North, but the better comparison is with Amsterdam. It is fitting that the Hermitage should hold some of the very best Rembrandts, including my favourite, "The Return of the Prodigal Son". In Moscow, snow in winter is just another hardship to be endured; in St. Petersburg it adds to the enchantment. In mid-winter I have walked along the banks of the frozen Neva and watched people standing bare-chested to catch the pale rays of the low sun. I have also been there during the "white nights" in June, when at midnight sitting on a park bench one can still read the headlines of a newspaper.

St. Petersburg has survived many challenges (and changes of name). From September 1941 to January 1944 the city (then "Leningrad") was surrounded and bombarded by German forces. The memory of that terrible conflict was not distant: visiting the excellent museum of Russian art, I was asked at the entrance if I had fought in "the war". "Which war?" I asked. "The war of 1941" was the reply; for Russians, the war started in that year, not in 1939. Apparently if I had been a soldier then, even in the British forces, I would have qualified for reduced-price entry. (Would I have got it if I had been in the German army? – the conversation was in Russian and the lady at the ticket-office probably could not guess which foreign country I came from.)

There was poverty in St. Petersburg too, though less in evidence than on the streets of Moscow. Once, in a small park just off the Nevsky Prospekt, I was approached by an elderly, respectable-looking man. He asked if he could show me his art-work, which he carried in a folder and was hoping to sell. It turned out that he was a retired teacher, trying like so many others to eke out a living on a pension much reduced by inflation.

Kiev, capital of Ukraine, is much less well known. Orthodoxy spread from Kiev into Russia and one is very conscious of that tradition; the cathedral in particular is splendid. Ukraine had suffered perhaps even more than Russia from economic collapse, and at the time of my visits was struggling to establish its own institutions. There were very few tourists; indeed the city would have been quite unprepared to receive them in any numbers. At the end of one of my visits I had to make my own way to the airport. No taxi would take me: they did not have enough petrol for the journey (about 30 km.) There was an airport bus, but this, being likewise short of fuel, would leave only when it had at least twenty passengers. But then, I said, I might miss my plane. There was a solution: if time was pressing, one could hire the entire bus... How much would that cost? – not much more than a taxi in a western city. In fact, enough people turned up, so I got to the airport in plenty of time.

At the airport, several Tupolevs formerly belonging to Aeroflot were sitting idle with covers over their engines. Ukraine had just got its own airline, using a brand-new leased Airbus. The plane was almost empty, and I was upgraded to first-class where I was the only passenger. There were three or four very beautiful hostesses with nothing much to do but very keen to improve their English; I was also invited into the pilot's cabin. It was the most enjoyable flight of my life...

After negotiations which had lasted in some cases since 1994, on 1 May 2004 the European Union was enlarged from 15 to 25 Member States by the accession of Estonia, Latvia, Lithuania, Poland, the Czech Republic, Slovakia, Hungary, and Slovenia; also Cyprus and Malta. Bulgaria and Romania followed on 1 January 2007, taking the total to 27. [5]

On 1 May 2004, the accession day of the first ten of the above countries, a festival was held at the Parc du Cinquantenaire in Brussels. A huge EU flag flew under the ceremonial archway, the weather was fine, and it was a joyful occasion which attracted many people of various nationalities. All Member States but one had a stall. That one was the United Kingdom, once again missing a trick in the European game. Its slot had been filled by the Scottish Farmers Union, doing a good trade by cooking and selling steaks of prime Scottish beef. Other stalls offered a variety of attractive food, drink and other goods. When I went to get a Czech beer, it was sold out; no matter, I crossed the path and had a Polish beer instead. Romania and Bulgaria, not yet EU members, had stalls in a nearby park.

---

[1] The title "PHARE" came from the French *"Pologne-Hongrie: aide à la restructuration économique"* – and *phare* in French means "lighthouse"). The Commission has generally tried to invent meaningful names for its programmes, with greater or less success. In this case, as the programme was extended to other countries, the original meaning was lost. And curious pronunciations appeared in some languages of the region.

The initial aim was to help the countries concerned in a period of massive economic restructuring and political change. As several of them applied for membership of the EU, increased emphasis was placed on strengthening public administrations and institutions to function effectively inside the European Union and promoting convergence with EU legislation (*the acquis communautaire*). In 1999 a "Special Accession Programme for Agriculture and Rural Development" (SAPARD) took over rural and agricultural development, aiming to help the adjustment on accession to the Common Agricultural Policy.

[2] Since geographic Europe is considered to extend to the Urals (placing its centre in western Ukraine), several countries – especially Poland, former Czechoslovakia, Hungary – dislike being referred to as "Eastern Europe". As contacts with the European institutions developed following the upheavals of 1999, the abbreviation "CEECs" came into general use.

[3] The role of young women is an interesting aspect of the post-1989 reforms, and I formed my own thesis on the matter. In many offices, a boss from the old regime – who would probably know no foreign language other than Russian – would need to recruit staff with other language skills. Young women may have been more likely to meet this requirement. Initially, their tasks might have been limited to translating letters and handling phone calls: but whoever manages communications soon knows all about the activities of the office. Some bosses of the old school would try to resist them; more sensible ones would take advantage of their skills. So before long, these young workers would get responsibilities well above the norm for their age.

As an instance of this: in the mid-1990s two very able young women – Agata Zdanowicz and Iwona Lisztwan – were employed under the PHARE programme in an advisory capacity to the Polish Ministry of Agriculture.

(Both these, like staff in the Policy Advisory Unit in Bucharest, had been recruited by a consultant, Graham Dalton from Aberdeen University, who had a flair for talent-spotting.) A couple of years later, Agata was appointed a Director in the Ministry, until a political change forced her out. Both have subsequently pursued interesting careers; both now have responsible positions with the European Commission in Brussels.

[4] It was interesting that the preferred language for this seminar in Bucharest was English – I had expected French, given the Latin origins of Romanian. All over Europe, and of course in the world at large, French has been losing ground. In Brussels when I arrived in 1973, French dominated – I have already referred to the secret document wherein Edward Heath agreed that British appointees to European institutions would use French; on first contact with an official or a secretary, one would automatically speak French.

However, each successive enlargement has brought new staff from countries where English is now the first foreign language taught in schools – the Scandinavian countries, obviously, but also the Central/Eastern European countries, even Romania. Personally, being comfortable in French, I see reasons to regret this trend; one result will be a corresponding decline in knowledge of French culture and literature. But for the modern world a world language is needed, and that presently is English – or rather, the various forms of speech to which English has adapted in different parts of the world.

[5] The big omissions in this list of new Member States are of course the components of the former Yugoslavia, other than Slovenia. Since Marshal Tito had broken off relations with the Soviet Union, it had developed closer links with the West. It also benefited economically from tourism along the Dalmatian coast. Unfortunately, the wars provoked by declarations of independence on the part of several of the constituent republics and then by ethnic strife in Kosovo kept the region apart from the general European movement towards integration. However, since 2003 the European Union has a programme of co-operation with the "Western Balkans", and most of the new countries have applied or will soon apply for membership. See next chapter.

IX. WHITHER EUROPE ?

The European Community, now the European Union, has grown from six to twenty-seven. To adapt the EU institutions to this enlargement and to reinforce the EU's position in world affairs, the new "Lisbon Treaty" entered into force on 1 December 2009.

Meanwhile, "euro-sceptic" tendencies have become more marked. In the United Kingdom, the coalition government formed in May 2010 contains elements on both sides of this debate.

Important issues relating to further enlargement, immigration policy and other matters lie ahead.

Russia still has not established a stable democratic system and its economy remains unbalanced. Its relations with its neighbours are conflictual and its role in the world is uncertain.

I ceased my professional work on 1 January 2000, and since then have not travelled so much around Europe. However, while keeping a base in Belgium and thus maintaining a few valued contacts in EU circles, I have come frequently to Andalucia, learning to appreciate the sophisticated Moorish civilisation which reigned in this area for some seven centuries, till the fall of Granada to the "Catholic Monarchs" in 1492. If Moslem armies had not been turned back at Poitiers in 732, Islam might have come to dominate in much of Western Europe.

The civilisation of al-Andalus far surpassed anything further north in Europe, and for most of the time it tolerated Jews and Christians. It created such wonders as the Great Mosque in Cordoba and the Alhambra in Granada. Cordoba was the greatest centre of learning in Europe; the works of the ancient Greek philosophers and scientists first reached western scholars through Arabic translations made in Baghdad and further translated in Cordoba into Latin and Hebrew.

In the Alpujarra, a long valley lying just below the peaks of the Sierra Nevada, the Moors created a network of irrigation channels which remains in use today, fed by springs rising from the snow-melt of the mountains above, and making this a beautiful, verdant valley dotted with "white villages" of Moorish origin. In one of these I now have a little house to which I can come whenever I feel inclined.

This is not a bad vantage-point from which to observe some of the effects of the opening-up of Europe. Spanish rural areas had been doubly cut off and disadvantaged: by the civil war and its aftermath under Franco, and by the dictator's deliberate neglect of rural areas, a potential source of trouble (guerrillas continued to operate in the Andalucian mountains until 1951). Two factors have brought immense changes: Spain entered the European Union in 1986, becoming eligible for EU funds, and tourism has vastly increased.

Not all these effects are positive. While tourism has created much employment, anarchic development along the coasts has had disastrous social and ecological consequences. But Spain has on the whole made good use of EU funds, building spectacular motorways over mostly barren mountain-sides and creating badly-needed dams; rural tourism has also been promoted by EU money.

When the euro was introduced on 1 January 2002, replacing national currencies, I wondered how the village shopkeepers would manage. In fact, the transition was remarkably smooth. At first, goods were still priced in pesetas and the total bill was converted into euros. Then prices were shown in both currencies; the village church installed two collection boxes, one for each currency. Gradually the pesetas were dropped, though for some time large amounts (such as house prices) continued to be quoted in millions of pesetas. Now I can even use my Belgian bank card to pay for groceries in the village shop. In principle, I should be able to transfer money between Belgian and Spanish bank accounts without charge, though my Spanish bank does not seem to have heard of this rule.

At the time of writing, the euro has been adopted by twelve of the fifteen "old" EU Member States (Denmark, Sweden and the United Kingdom being the exceptions) and by four of the ten latest arrivals (Cyprus, Malta, Slovakia and Slovenia); Montenegro and Kosovo, though not yet even in line for EU membership, also use the euro as their official currency. The advantages for travellers are obvious; so are the benefits to trade and commerce of all kinds, as the single currency facilitates transactions and removes currency risk from investments within the zone.

During the global financial crisis of 2008–9, the euro and its management by the European Central Bank averted currency crises for the individual eurozone countries (causing Iceland to think it might do better inside the EU and with the euro). But for the weaker economies, currency stability comes at the price of a difficult adjustment to overcome subsequent recession.

The problems of Greece in particular, with huge public debts and current deficits, underlined the difficulty of trying to operate a monetary union without economic union or effective controls. Germany remains attached to the principle that each country in the European Monetary Union must keep its own house in order. It was agreed, with some difficulty, that Greece would receive funds both from the International Monetary Fund and from its eurozone partners.

As the crisis deepened to threaten other countries — especially Portugal and Spain – and the euro itself, on 9-10 May 2010 a much bigger rescue package was agreed: it totals €750 billion, mostly in loan guarantees financed by the eurozone countries and Sweden and Poland, plus loans from the International Monetary Fund. (Britain refused to contribute, so should not expect help if it cannot solve its own financial difficulties.) The aid is available to any eurozone country but conditional on strict fiscal restraints, supervised by the IMF. Moreover, the European Central Bank departed from its usual caution by providing support to financial markets through the purchase of government bonds.

The remarkable thing about this relief package, apart from its size, is that it was agreed at all, over one hectic weekend: prime ministers meeting in Brussels on the Saturday, finance ministers on the Sunday, with agreement at 3 a.m. on the Monday morning. It largely corresponds to French objectives, as a potential step towards eurozone "economic governance". The German chancellor, Angela Merkel, showed statesmanship in overriding both political opposition at home and her own previously-expressed objections.

The necessary austerity measures in several countries will be fiercely resisted, and there will be further difficult discussions on Commission proposals to strengthen mutual surveillance of the national budgets of eurozone countries. Countries wanting to join the eurozone (if they still wish to do so) must expect to be subjected to much closer scrutiny than was applied to Greece; Estonia is at the head of the queue.

Still, as Tony Barber, the Brussels correspondent of the *Financial Times,* wrote on 11 May: "It is foolish to underestimate the determination of EU leaders not to jeopardise 53 years of peaceful European co-operation". José Manuel Barroso, President of the Commission, said: "The history of European integration confirms that sometimes it is only under extreme pressure that governments make these kinds of hard choices".

At the personal level the other big advantage of the EU is ease of travel within the "Schengen" area, covering all the present Member States except Britain and Ireland. A traveller should be able to move without hindrance from the Arctic Circle in Scandinavia to the south of Italy, Portugal or Spain. When Romania and Bulgaria are admitted to the zone, it will be possible to go through them with no border control as far as Athens. Iceland, Norway and Switzerland, though not EU members, likewise participate fully in Schengen.

I have always attached great importance to education, so I see the Erasmus programme, enabling thousands of young people to study outside their countries of origin, as one of the most useful EU initiatives.

Though I studied economics, I am not one of those who regard "Gross National Product" as a sufficient indicator of welfare; nevertheless, I am convinced that people in Western Europe today can have far better lives than was possible some fifty years ago. Economic growth would have happened anyway, but it has been greatly facilitated by the central element of the EU since its inception, the "common market", i.e. free trade within the area and a common external tariff, complemented now by freedom to take work in other EU countries.

Free trade calls for common rules of competition, to avoid distortion by State aids or discriminatory national regulations: this is an area where the European Commission, backed up when necessary by the European Court of Justice, plays a vital role. Many people object to such EU rules: undoubtedly there has been overregulation, especially in the early stages, but the Commission has become more cautious in this respect and – as will be seen below – the principles of "subsidiarity" and "proportionality" have been reinforced. The Commission's powers to regulate cross-border mergers and takeovers are very necessary to prevent the emergence of monopolies in this age of "globalisation".

The Lisbon Treaty and its consequences

What lies ahead for the European Union? Anything I write today will soon be overtaken by events, but perhaps some comments will at least serve as bench-marks. The recent passage of the Lisbon Treaty – it entered into force on 1 December 2009 – provides food for thought.

The Treaty of Rome of 1957 provided a relatively simple and balanced system: the Commission would propose legislation, the European Parliament would be consulted, the Council of Ministers (representing Member States) would decide, and the Commission would implement the result.

This structure already contained potential problems: in particular, how would the Council take its decisions? The Rome Treaty said: by "qualified majority" (i.e. votes weighted roughly according to the size of each Member State). This soon hit the opposition of France under de Gaulle, leading to the "Luxembourg compromise", under which a country should not be overruled on a matter of "vital national interest". Difficult and protracted negotiations were needed to reach agreement.

With additional functions and above all with the expansion in membership, the problem of decision-making, or more broadly that of the governance of the Union, has become more acute. Hence the perceived need for new rules.

The passage was long and fraught with difficulties: the first attempt, aiming at a single "Constitutional Treaty", was rejected by referenda in France and the Netherlands. It was then necessary to find an alternative different enough to be adopted by parliamentary process in those two countries but not so different as to require re-ratification in the countries which had accepted the first proposal.

The result, which ultimately became the "Lisbon Treaty", was initially turned down by the Irish public and only accepted after concessions to meet Irish concerns. All this is described in other sources; I have myself posted a commentary on Internet, so I can be briefer here.[1] Suffice it to say that as a result of the Lisbon Treaty, the two basic acts remain – the Treaty on European Union and the Treaty on the Functioning of the European Union (this previously replaced the Treaty of Rome) – but they have undergone important amendments. In particular:

- A post of "European President" was created. The main function is to chair meetings of the European Council – i.e. the gatherings of Heads of State and Government. The original intention of promoters was to provide a single authority at the head of the Union. In fact, this European President does not have real powers: to get anything done, he must ask the traditional Council (of Ministers), or the Commission, whose President will be jealous of his prerogatives.

  Moreover, the six-monthly "rotating presidency" continues at the level of the ministerial Councils (except for external affairs), and the leader of the country holding that post may not have the same priorities as the European President.[2] Clearly, the European President will need considerable powers of persuasion. The first appointee, the Belgian Herman van Rompuy, is an accomplished politician with a quiet but forceful personality, who may make a success of his job, but it will not be easy.

- A very important new post is that of "High Representative of the Union for Foreign Affairs and Security Policy". This HR presides over the ministerial Council for External Affairs; oddly, she is also a Vice-President of the Commission. Consequently, the HR is in a potentially powerful position. The surprise appointee, the British life peer Catherine Ashton, only recently appointed to a Commission post (for trade), had little foreign affairs experience but has considerable personality. She certainly has a great (and unexpected) opportunity, if she can avoid getting bogged down in an administrative morass.

- Further, the High Representative is to be assisted by a European External Action Service (EAAS). This is expected to be a large body: some 5000 officials, drawn from EU institutions and from member states. Incredibly, the Treaty is vague about its purpose and left open its organisation and functioning; its establishment is proving problematic.

- With one Commissioner per Member State, the Commission has become much too large. So the Lisbon Treaty envisaged that the number should be reduced. But some countries, especially Ireland, objected to the idea that at some periods they would not have a Commissioner, so this proposal was dropped.

- To facilitate decision-making in the Council, voting by "qualified majority" became the standard procedure. But there are provisions – not unlike the former so-called "Luxembourg compromise" – which could enable a minority of countries to hold up a decision.

- The Lisbon Treaty reinforced existing provisions requiring Council deliberations to be held "in public". The principle is admirable, but Ministers are unlikely to make major concessions in open session.[3]

- The European Parliament has been given increased powers, including the role of "co-decision" with the Council in an extended number of areas. These include agricultural policy: a step which could open the door to even greater pressures from powerful farm lobbies. Moreover, this is a very complicated and potentially lengthy procedure.
  On the other hand, the European Parliament itself has little popular support: in elections in June 2009, only 43% of the potential electorate turned out, and participation was particularly low among young people.

- The Lisbon Treaty provides for consultations between the European institutions and national parliaments. Among other matters, the latter will be able to check if "subsidiarity and proportionality" (in other words, not doing at the Union level anything that can be done lower down the scale, and not doing more than is necessary) are being properly applied. The principle of consultation is welcome, but its application seems liable to cause further delays in enacting legislation.

Do these changes – and others which I have not mentioned here – make the EU more effective in its decision-making and more democratic? This is doubtful: the outcome resembles the camel that must have been designed by a committee. Indeed, many committees were involved and there were many different points of view. As a result, provisions aimed at greater efficiency are counterbalanced by others aimed at curtailing any excessive centralisation of power.

What seems to have been overlooked – even in creating the ambitious EAAS – is that the strength of the European Union in world affairs depends above all on whether it has common European policies on major issues. It does have some such agreed positions. The EU has taken a lead on climate change; it also has an apparently firm position on the Middle East, opposing further Israeli settlements on Palestinian territory (so had President Obama, but he has a powerful pro-Israeli lobby to contend with). One test of the new arrangements may be whether the EU can exert greater influence over that very intractable problem.

There was little discussion anywhere of the real issues posed by the Lisbon Treaty. Few people ever knew much about its contents. In itself, it was unreadable, since it consisted of amendments to previous Treaties. As a result, the proposal provoked many objections, some of which were unfounded: opponents could declare that it will have such-and-such undesirable consequences without much fear of contradiction.

The troubled passage of the Treaty has an important consequence: it shows that it has become extremely difficult to get the European public to approve new EU legislation. This does not have much to do with the contents of the proposals: in each of the national referenda where the initial "Constitutional Treaty" (France, Netherlands) and later the Lisbon Treaty (Ireland) was turned down, this was largely due to domestic issues and to protest votes against the national government; if a referendum had been called in some other countries, particularly the UK, the result there would probably also have been negative.

This has the important implication that no further treaty amendments are likely to be proposed for a long time to come. Maybe this will not matter so much where EU internal affairs are concerned; the big decisions – rightly or wrongly – have been taken. But it may matter for the EU's external relations: in particular this problem puts a question-mark on further accessions to the EU if these have to be submitted to referendum.

A two-speed Community?

There are no easy ways to manage a community of twenty-seven or more countries. With such a large Union, it is inevitable that some countries will want to move forward faster than others. So the idea of a "two-speed" community has been much discussed: this was taken up in previous treaties (Amsterdam 1999 and Nice 2001) under the more diplomatic title of "enhanced cooperation" and was retained under the Lisbon Treaty.

This procedure would allow a group of Member States (a minimum of nine is required) to act on their own, as has happened with the euro and the Schengen agreement. The idea is anathema to convinced federalists, and carries the risk of disintegration of the EU, so it is subject to safeguards: it must be approved by the Commission (and the European Parliament in areas of "co-decision" – see above) and by a qualified majority of all Member States. It is to be seen as a last resort, when normal procedures have been exhausted, and only in specified fields including security and justice; its application to divorce law is under discussion.

The British problem

Having followed the course of Britain's relations with the European Community/Union since the time the Treaty of Rome was signed, I find it sad that Britain is still – to say the least – uncertain of its role. From the start, Britain seems to have got everything wrong. By withdrawing from the early negotiations on the creation of the European Economic Community, it deprived itself of any influence in its constitution. By setting up instead EFTA with six small northern countries, it achieved little of value but antagonised the EEC leaders.

When later British governments changed course and applied for EEC membership, they first courted outright rejection (by President de Gaulle), then had to accept unfavourable, almost humiliating terms – in particular with regard to trade with the Commonwealth, budgetary provisions, the common agricultural policy and fisheries.

Then, just one year after a Conservative government took Britain into the European Community in 1973, a newly-elected Labour government demanded a "renegotiation" and conducted a referendum on the results, which it stage-managed to produce a favourable but unconvincing result. Subsequently, Britain's standing was further reduced by Margaret Thatcher's prolonged and aggressive demands for a better budget deal. In the end, she got some satisfaction, but earned no goodwill.

Britain remains outside both the eurozone and the Schengen area. One can be in favour of both these developments without necessarily advocating UK participation in either. The pound does have a role as an international currency, and having no land frontier with other countries (other than that between Northern Ireland and the Irish Republic, which is also outside Schengen) the maintenance of border controls perhaps does not matter so much. The main issues lie elsewhere.

The Labour government under Tony Blair promised to "put Britain at the heart of Europe" but did little to achieve this. Meanwhile, the political line-up of 1973 has been inversed: it is now in the Conservative Party that "euro-scepticism" prevails. In the European Parliament it has removed itself from the centre-right European People's Party group to form the much more right-wing and "anti-federalist" European Conservative and Reformist group.

Moreover, both the United Kingdom Independence Party and the far-right, racist British National Party, who share the aim of taking Britain out of the EU, have gained seats in local elections and even in the European Parliament; fortunately, as they hold none in the national parliament their influence is limited.

The Conservative Party under David Cameron gained the most seats in the national election of May 2010. The Party does not demand with-drawal from the EU (though some of its supporters would probably like this). However, its manifesto for the election declared that "the steady and unaccountable intrusion of the European Union into almost every aspect of our lives has been made worse by the Lisbon Treaty".

Having less than an absolute majority in Parliament, the Conserva-tives have formed a coalition with the Liberal Democrats. The "Lib Dems" have always promoted Britain's participation in the EU, and their present leader, Nick Clegg, has strong European credentials, un-precedented for a British political leader: study at the College of Europe in Bruges, a period within the European Commission, another as a member of the European Parliament. He speaks several languages and has a Spanish wife (also a former College of Europe student); their children have Spanish names.

The compromise agreement on which the coalition has been founded starts by declaring that Britain will be a "positive participant" in the EU. But from then on, it seems to lean much more in the Conservative direction: there should be no further transfer of sovereignty or powers to the EU, and any future draft Treaty that might do so would be subjected to referendum (which, given the state of public opinion, is tantamount to rejection). Britain would not join the euro – but that is hardly an issue at present. (See full text in end-note [4])

This text does at least remove for the life of this Parliament the option of withdrawal from the EU (envisaged by the Lisbon Treaty), which would be sad for Europe and bad for the UK. Even supposing that the political and legal obstacles could be overcome, some kind of association or trade agreement would have to be negotiated and Britain would not get favourable terms. Moreover, Britain would suffer further loss of influence in Europe and in the world: in particular, despite British claims of a "special relationship", American leaders would have little interest in a Britain outside the European Union.

However, as the euphoria of the coalition agreement evaporates, difficulties between the partners are bound to arise, especially as other EU countries try to reinforce their co-operation in various fields (as recommended *inter alia* in the report to the European Council in May 2010 by the "Reflection Group" of twelve "wise men").[5] Will the UK under the coalition government be in permanent opposition? That is certainly not what the Lib Dems wanted. There can be argument as to what constitutes a "transfer of sovereignty or powers". And there are bound to be new initiatives which the Conservatives will resist but the Lib Dems want to support: how are such conflicts to be resolved? It seems that Britain will continue to be an awkward partner in the EU.

The new EU Member States

The recent accessions of ten countries from the former Soviet-controlled zone have happened faster and on the whole more easily than anyone could have foreseen. The Baltic countries, once part of the Russian Empire, had been independent states with close ties to the western world from 1920 until 1939, when they were annexed by the Soviet Union. Even under Soviet rule, many of their people had maintained contacts with relatives and friends in Western Europe or North America and – very important – many had a good knowledge of English or other western languages. So their adaptation was rapid and their living standards rose quickly (at least, until the global financial crisis of 2008/9). Their entry into the European Union has been relatively easy.

The same, by and large, can be said for Poland, the Czech Republic, Hungary, Slovakia and Slovenia, despite their economic and political difficulties. Now they are all participating effectively in the EU (although the Czech government mismanaged its first turn in the presidency role and President Klaus' efforts to derail the Lisbon Treaty did not add to the country's standing with its EU partners).

Romania and Bulgaria, probably because they had suffered from particularly repressive and demoralising dictatorships, have had greater difficulties. At the time of writing, the Commission has suspended some of the aid due to Bulgaria until that country manages to deal more effectively with corruption in its administration and judiciary.

Overall, the experience with the eastern enlargement of the European Union has been highly beneficial to both sides (I am omitting Malta and Cyprus of which I have no knowledge). The opportunities it offered were due to peoples who had found themselves on the wrong side of the Iron Curtain, and who for some four decades while the West was prospering had suffered from oppressive regimes and mismanaged economies.

Fears in the west of a massive movement of workers who would undermine the labour market – the French in particular had a phobia about the anticipated "Polish plumber" – have proved largely unfounded.

Some EU countries placed restrictions on immigration from the new Member States; the United Kingdom and Ireland, which did not do so, received much larger numbers than expected and there are undoubtedly areas where a big influx has caused problems.

On the whole, workers from the central and eastern European countries have filled jobs where they were needed, and as income levels rise in the new Member States a new balance is being reached: already in countries like Poland, plumbers and other tradesmen are in short supply. With fertility rates among the indigenous population below the minimum replacement rate in Eastern Europe as well as in the west, immigration within the enlarged Union is unlikely to be a major problem in the longer term.[6]

Further enlargement?
To join the European Union, a candidate country must be a European State and must meet three criteria: [7]

- political: stability of institutions guaranteeing democracy, the rule of law, human rights and respect for and protection of minorities;
- economic: existence of a functioning market economy and the capacity to cope with competitive pressure and market forces within the Union;
- acceptance of the existing Community legislation and practice (the *acquis communautaire*): ability to take on the obligations of member-ship, including adherence to the aims of political, economic and monetary union.

Iceland – once it recovers from its financial collapse of 2008 – should easily meet these criteria, and may or may not decide to enter. When its currency suddenly lost two-thirds of its value at the outset of the economic crisis of 2008-09, the euro and the EU began to look attractive. The subsequent problems in the eurozone may lead to a change of heart, or the population may change its mind when it discovers what terms it can get, particularly on fisheries.

In due course the EU will no doubt gather up most of the missing countries in the Western Balkans, starting probably with Croatia. But it is not so long since the disintegration of Yugoslavia provoked ethnic conflict. In Bosnia-Herzegovina and in Kosovo, the EU was unable on its own to impose a peaceful solution and US armed might had to be called in. Certainly, cruise missiles and air attacks were able to crush Serbia into submission; but Serbian nationalism has ancient roots and remains very much alive. The government of Bosnia-Herzegovina is dysfunctional and an uneasy truce between the ethnic communities is maintained only by the international Peace Implementation Council and its High Representative, whose mandate has been extended beyond the original time-frame. Serbia (with support from Russia) refuses to recognise Kosovo's self-proclaimed independence and will no doubt maintain this position unless forced to abandon it in the context of its own application to join the EU.

Looking further afield, the Ukraine, with virtually no experience of being independent let alone democratic, is still struggling to establish a stable political system and a viable economy. Throughout most of its history the country has been in the Russian orbit; its language is as close to Russian as, say, Dutch is to German; Kiev is the cradle of Eastern Orthodoxy. In the eastern regions most of the people speak Russian and are politically pro-Russian. Ukraine's dependence on Russian oil and gas means that it remains under the thumb of Moscow.

Former President Yushchenko was eliminated in the first round of the presidential election of January 2010: this mainly underlined the failed hopes of the Orange Revolution of 2004/5, but he was also the main advocate for membership of both the EU and NATO. In the second round, the acrimonious tussle between Yulia Timoschenko and Viktor Yanukovitch led to the victory of the latter. All the provinces in the east and south of the country, including the mining and industrial Donbas region and Crimea, returned majorities for Yanukovitch; Kiev and all the rural provinces of the north and west voted for Timoshenko.

Yanukovitch has been regarded as pro-Russian, and his most important act following his election has been to make a highly controversial deal with Russia whereby Ukraine receives gas on preferential terms but Russia gets a lease on the naval base at Sebastopol until 2042. It remains to be seen whether he will bring about the desirable balance in Ukraine's relations as between Russia and the EU. And the country's standing in the world may turn in part on success or failure in organising (with Poland) the 2012 European football championship.

Moldova is torn ethnically and linguistically between its Slavic (partly Russian) and Latin (Romanian) elements; it remains politically unstable. In the Transnistria region, which demands independence, Russia maintains a strong military presence. Like the Ukraine, Moldova is included in the European Union's "Neighbourhood Policy", but its chances of EU membership seem remote.[8]

Belarus fulfils none of the conditions for membership and will not do so until the authoritarian rule of President Alexander Lukashenko is over. It is not even in the Council of Europe (the only European country that is not a member).

Where does Europe end at its south-eastern corner? – somewhere along the Carpathians, but there is no clear border-line. Georgia under

President Saakashvili is very anxious to ally itself with the West, is covered by the EU Neighbourhood Policy and is a member of the Council of Europe. So are Armenia and Azerbaijan, but it is difficult to imagine any of these countries fitting into the EU in the foreseeable future.[9]

The really difficult issue is, of course, Turkey. Whatever public opinion may think, the EU has never officially questioned Turkey's status as a European State (in 1987 its initial application for membership was accepted while that from Morocco was turned down as that country was clearly not European). Turkey has an educated and Western-oriented elite; Istanbul – the former Constantinople – is a European "capital of culture" in 2010. Nevertheless, most of Turkey's land mass is in Asia, likewise its large rural population, which knows little or nothing of European history and culture.

For a long time Turkey has been left in the expectation that in due course it can become a member of the EU. A customs union with the EU was established in 1995; in 1999 Turkey was granted "candidate status"; an Accession Partnership was agreed in 2001. But accession negotiations began only in 2005 and are currently blocked, mainly over the Cyprus problem and issues concerning freedom of speech. It might have been better to tell Turkey from the start that while it is welcome to the most favourable trade and aid arrangements possible, it should not expect full membership.

There are strong practical obstacles. Turkey has a population of 75 million, less at present than Germany which has 83 million but more than any other EU country – France, Italy and the UK are each around 60 million. Moreover, while European populations are falling, Turkish population is rising: by about 2016 it will overtake Germany.[10] Consequently, Turkey would be entitled to a relatively large weighting in Council votes and a correspondingly large number of MEPs. On the other hand, as a relatively poor country with a large rural sector qualifying for aids under the common agricultural policy, it would be a substantial net beneficiary under the EU budget – which of course has always been the main reason for Turkey's candidacy but which could prove an excessive burden to the EU.

The motives for opening the door to Turkey have been mainly strategic. Turkey is a vital NATO partner, and the United States has continually urged the EC/EU to accept it. EU leaders are divided on the issue, some preferring a "privileged partnership". As their electorates – who in some countries would be consulted by referendum – are mainly opposed, fearing mass immigration, it remains difficult to see how Turkey could gain entry, other than in a context in which Europe's security was seriously threatened.

Immigration

The immigration issue has been approached by different Member States in various ways. So while the EU has free movement of people within its boundary, it has no common immigration policy.

The EU needs immigrant labour, as its own native population is falling; without an influx of younger workers, the cost of social security systems will be borne by a decreasing number of contributors. This issue has been stressed by the high-level "Reflection Group", already mentioned, which declared:

"The combination of ageing populations and a contracting domestic labour force is set to have drastic consequences for Europe. Left unchecked, it will translate into unsustainable pressure on pension, health and welfare systems, and into negative outcomes for economic growth and taxation." [11]

Besides this domestic consideration, the EU – as one of the world's richest regions – clearly has a responsibility towards the relief of over-population, underemployment and poverty in other parts of the world. The pressures will remain great in view of the huge gap in living standards between Third World countries and Europe – maybe also through consequences of climate change such as the flooding of a large area of Bangladesh. Aid programmes are important but are not the only solution.

A coherent EU immigration policy is badly needed, but will not be easy. There is not much public support, and the most difficult issue arises over Islamic migrants. Estimates vary: there are probably between twenty and thirty million Moslems living in EU countries – only some 4–6% of the total EU population, but being concentrated in specific urban areas their impact appears greater. Their number will increase, both by natural growth – the birth-rate among Moslems is much higher than in the native European populations – and by further immigration.

To what extent can the EU accept more Islamic immigrants without undermining its own cultural values? The Treaty on European Union, as amended by the Lisbon Treaty, states (Article 3.3) that the Union "shall respect its rich cultural and linguistic diversity, and shall ensure that Europe's cultural heritage is safeguarded and enhanced". That seems to imply that immigrants should be assimilated rather than develop their own separate communities. But in many areas where there are numerous Moslems, they quite naturally prefer to live among themselves.

There is bound to be continued friction over Muslim practices, in particular the wearing of *burkas* – or the treatment of women in general – and the construction of mosques and minarets. And it is difficult to see how "Sharia law" can co-exist with the long-established laws of European countries, despite some utterances to the contrary.

The columnist Christopher Caldwell has written a well-documented analysis of the effects of Islamic immigration, with the sub-title "Can Europe be the same with different people in it?" He concludes:

"It is certain that Europe will emerge changed from its confrontation with Islam. It is far less certain that Islam will prove assimilable. Europe finds itself in a contest with Islam for the allegiance of its newcomers. For now, Islam is the stronger party in that contest, in an obvious demographic way and in a less obvious philosophical way." (p. 286)

By the latter, Caldwell means that the confidence of Muslim believers is likely to prevail over the uncertain religious views of most Europeans. So policies based on mutual tolerance are likely to be to the disadvantage of the Europeans.[12]

This is an uncomfortable conclusion. I recalled at the outset of this chapter that a thousand years ago the most advanced and tolerant civilisation in Europe was that of Islamic Spain, until it was crushed by a particularly intolerant Catholic monarchy. Most religions (Buddhism is an exception) go through a fundamentalist phase, which may last a long time. Our perceptions of Islam at present are unfortunately shaped by the actions of Islamic extremists, though this is unfair to the vast majority of Moslems living in Europe.

Our continent has already changed dramatically during my lifetime; it will continue to change, and no doubt the role of Moslems in European society will be an important factor in this process.

Overall, we can look back with some satisfaction on what has been achieved. Most people in the European Union live far better than their grandparents or even their parents did. At last, the western side of the continent is at peace – though only just. The Balkans have barely emerged from the conflicts that resulted from the break-up of Yugoslavia; the newest entities, Bosnia and Kosovo especially, remain fragile. At the regional level, the troubles in Northern Ireland are close to solution; Basque terrorism has been tamed though not yet crushed.

Russia today

Russia and the other European countries share much of their culture. Our music would be poorer without Tchaikovsky, Mussorgsky, Rachmaninoff or Stravinsky. If we find Tolstoy or Dostoyevsky heavy going, anyone can enjoy the plays of Chekhov. Russian painters are less well-known, apart from Chagall who spent most of his life in France: one needs to go to Moscow and St. Petersburg to see most of the great works of Levitan, Repin and others. The ceremonies of the Russian Orthodox church may seem unduly florid, but its churches (now restored) are beautiful and its vocal musical tradition is glorious.

Nevertheless, Russia still seems a different world, even after the fall of Communism. In 1991, no-one in Russia had experience of democracy nor of a market economy. So it is sad for the Russian people who had already suffered so much, but it was probably inevitable, that the abuses of the communist system were replaced by others. A former British ambassador to Moscow has written:

"Russia remains introverted, nationalistic, distrusted by its neighbours, unsure of itself and its place in the world. It never had much chance of making the comparatively rapid and easy transition to democracy achieved in the rest of Europe". [13]

Indeed, Russia was not ready for "shock therapy". As already explained, the early effects of price liberalisation were dire and left a durable distrust of the market economy. Moreover, privatisation of former State-owned enterprises was badly bungled: coupons supposed to be distributed among citizens ended up in the hands of unscrupulous entrepreneurs and permitted the emergence of a privileged class of rich "New Russians". In this money-grabbing society, people in the professional classes on fixed salaries feel left out; some think that times were perhaps better under Communism. (See the interview between a Russian father and son in Annex II.)

I have already referred to the decline in life expectancy; alcohol and drug abuse is partly responsible, but the underlying cause is probably the economic distress felt by those left impoverished in the race for greater riches. The economy remains far too dependent on its oil and gas exports, and is thus exposed to fluctuating world prices.

Particularly disturbing for Russia's future is that it is falling behind in scientific research, as compared with China in particular but also Brazil, India and the USA. This reflects a big reduction in funding for research and development after the collapse of the Soviet Union, and an exodus of many scientists.[14]

There are obscure links between political leaders and business oligarchs. There is no effective parliamentary opposition. Though in principle free speech is permitted, those who criticise the regime are liable to suffer for it. The only independent television channel has been shut down. Insurrections in Chechnya, Ingushetia and Dagestan have been brutally repressed. Violence leads to violence, and now Russian civilians suffer from Caucasian terrorism: almost as I write these lines, two young women have blown themselves up in the Moscow metro along with dozens of passengers, apparently in revenge for the deaths of their husbands. Politically-motivated assassinations go unpunished, notably that in 2006 of Anna Politkovskaya, the journalist who had been criticising Russian actions in Chechnya. Russia is second only to Turkey in the number of human rights violations, most of which remain unpunished.[15]

With such lack of transparency, it is debatable whether Russia is yet a democracy. It is not even sure that democracy is what most of the people want: having never experienced it, they seem to prefer having a strong leader, a kind of Tsar for modern times, and Vladimir Putin fills that role. Yet no-one is quite sure which of the two, Putin (currently the Prime Minister) or Dmitry Medvedev (currently President), really governs the country, nor which will become the next President. Medvedev seems more open and forward-looking; he wrote in September 2009:

"An ineffective economy, semi-Soviet social sphere, weak democracy, negative demographic trends and an unstable Caucusus: these are very big problems even for a state like Russia." [16]

Some people in Russia are well aware of these problems. The Institute of Contemporary Development, set up to advise Medvedev, calls for a return to the system of electing regional governors and senators, practices that were abolished by Putin when he was President. It also calls for the Federal Security Service, the successor to the KGB, to be replaced by other institutions and for the media to be freed from state control. The *Financial Times* of 4 February 2010 commented that the report is "further evidence that a group of powerbrokers around Mr Medvedev is pushing the president to break ranks with his predecessor Mr Putin".

Russia and the EU countries have many interests in common, in both European and world affairs. For example, Serbia will not easily move to recognise Kosovo without Russian acquiescence. Seen from the West, Russia often appears uncooperative in international affairs, sometimes even aggressive. But Russian sensitivity has to be understood. With the break-up of the Soviet Union, Russia has lost an empire, and now most of its former vassal states have gone over to the European Union or want to do so.

It is to be hoped that the recently-appointed European President and especially the High Representative for external affairs will build a new and more constructive partnership with Russia. President Medvedev provided an opening in 2008 with a proposal for a new pan-European security treaty; this reflected Russia's dissatisfaction with the existing Organisation for Co-operation and Security in Europe. Only some EU countries have welcomed the proposal, and the USA has been cool to the idea, seen as potentially undermining NATO.

There are of course broader issues. All the ten countries formerly in the Soviet block which joined the European Union have also been admitted into NATO; so have Albania and Croatia; Georgia and the Ukraine have expressed interest, though the western powers have remained very cautious about this. [17]

From a Russian viewpoint, their country seems to become increasingly encircled by this NATO expansion. So Russia – particularly under Putin, whether as President or Prime Minister – has remained suspicious of western intentions. For this, of course, the West is also to blame, particularly in the misguided initiative by President George W. Bush to set up a missile defence system in the Czech Republic and Poland. This decision was reversed by President Barack Obama, raising hopes of a more sensitive US approach; but as these lines are being written it is announced that another base will be set up in Romania…

For the countries bordering Russia, still nervous about Russian intentions, membership of NATO has been at least as important a guarantee of their security as membership of the EU. Nevertheless, some of their citizens would have preferred their country to remain non-aligned, or even – dare one think it? – a reorganisation of the alliance to include Russia. Maybe an opportunity was missed in the early 1990s?

Until these security issues between Russia and the rest of Europe are fully resolved, Europe as a whole cannot be said to be united nor wholly at peace. In fact, a framework for co-operation has been created in the NATO-Russia Council. But NATO's title still reflects its "cold war" origins and its present purpose remains unclear; one can hardly expect Russia to co-operate enthusiastically. [18]

Obviously, progress on this front as on many others depends above all on the Americans, and much depends on President Obama. Inevitably, he has to juggle with numerous priorities, both domestic and international, and Europe may not be at the top of his list; he withdrew from a planned EU-US summit in Madrid in spring 2010. Fortunately, having obtained passage through Congress of the health bill, he seems to be devoting more attention to world issues, in particular arms control. In April 2010 Presidents Obama and Medvedev met in Prague to sign an important new Strategic Arms Reduction Treaty. Shortly afterwards, some forty world leaders held a summit in Washington aimed at keeping the world's nuclear materials out of the wrong hands. These at least are hopeful signs.

The European Union with twenty-seven Member States has a population of around 492 million. This is much less than China (1,354 mn.) or India (1,214 mn.) but more than the US (318 mn.). Its Gross Domestic Product is reckoned by the World Bank at some $16,553 billion, slightly more than that of the US ($14,204 bn.) and far more than China ($4,326 bn.) or India ($1,217 bn.). [19]

Russia's population is reckoned at 140 million, that of Ukraine at 45 mn., Belarus 10 mn. and Moldova 3.5 mn.

Consequently, if the EU speaks with a single voice, it should be able to carry significant weight in world affairs – all the more so if can act in concert with Russia.

The needs are great: consolidating the world economy after the crisis of 2008/9, alleviating the huge income gaps between rich and poor regions, confronting the challenge of climate change, dealing with terrorism, preventing further nuclear proliferation and above all averting the risk of some rogue state or terrorist group actually acquiring and using a nuclear weapon...

We can be grateful that at least within the European Union, twenty-seven nations have created links which make war between them inconceivable, showing that former enemies can work and progress together. In a troubled and dangerous world, that is surely worth having.

---

[1] As the Lisbon Treaty consists of amendments to previous treaties, it is indigestible to most readers. The "consolidated" text, incorporating these amendments to the Treaty on European Union and the Treaty on the Functioning of the European Union, can be found in the *Official Journal* (C83 of 30 March 2010) and on the Commission and Council websites; but these sources do not show where the changes have been made.

There is a good summary of the Treaty from a Luxembourg source: www.europaforum.public.lu, in four languages, and an Irish one: www. europaforum.public.lu. There is also an excellent account on *Wikipedia*: http://en.wikipedia.org/wiki/Lisbon_treaty.

My own contribution is on http://lisbontreatycommentary.wordpress.com.

[2] Following the Lisbon Treaty, the presidency of the ministerial Councils (other than that for Foreign Affairs) continues to rotate every six months, but is now shared by pre-established groups of three Member States, the two not actually in the chair being supposed to "assist the chair in all its responsibilities on the basis of a common programme". The first "trio" consists of Spain from 1 January 2010, followed by Belgium and Hungary. These three have established the requisite programme of "work priorities". Whether this procedure will be effective remains to be seen. The Spanish authorities do not seem to be giving up any significant responsibilities.

[3] The Lisbon Treaty declared that "The Council shall meet in public when it deliberates and votes on a draft legislative act..." i.e. in practice, on a Commission proposal. The requirement does not apply if the Council is

simply discussing, for example, a Commission communication (the logic of this is not evident). This does not mean that anyone can walk into the Council chamber: proceedings are relayed to a large space which is open to the public. It is also possible to view the proceedings, as well as press conferences and other events, on the Council's video system – http://video.consilium.europa.eu. In fact, a considerable effort has been made to render the decision-making process more transparent, and the Council Secretariat now has a substantial and effective information service. (I am grateful to Valerie Goldsmith and Dana Manescu in this service for explaining and demonstrating this to me.)

[4] The coalition text agreed between the Conservatives and the Liberal Democrats on 11 May 2010, in its section on the EU, reads:

"We agree that the British Government will be a positive participant in the European Union, playing a strong and positive role with our partners, with the goal of ensuring that all the nations of Europe are equipped to face the challenges of the 21st century: global competitiveness, global warming and global poverty.

"We agree that there should be no further transfer of sovereignty or powers over the course of the next Parliament. We will examine the balance of the EU's existing competences and will, in particular, work to limit the application of the Working Time Directive in the United Kingdom.

"We agree that we will amend the 1972 European Communities Act so that any proposed future Treaty that transferred areas of power, or competences, would be subject to a referendum on that Treaty – a 'referendum lock'. We will amend the 1972 European Communities Act so that the use of any passerelle would require primary legislation.

"We will examine the case for a United Kingdom Sovereignty Bill to make it clear that ultimate authority remains with Parliament.

"We agree that Britain will not join or prepare to join the Euro in this Parliament.

"We agree that we will strongly defend the UK's national interests in the forthcoming EU budget negotiations and that the EU budget should only focus on those areas where the EU can add value.

"We agree that we will press for the European Parliament only to have one seat, in Brussels.

"We agree that we will approach forthcoming legislation in the area of criminal justice on a case by case basis, with a view to maximising our country's security, protecting Britain's civil liberties and preserving the integrity of our criminal justice system. Britain will not participate in the establishment of any European Public Prosecutor."

This statement will be followed in due course by a final Coalition Agreement, covering the full range of policy and including foreign, defence and domestic policy issues not covered in this document.

[5] This "Reflection Group" – generally known as the twelve "wise men" – was set up by the European Council in December 2007 and submitted its report on 8 May 2010 (available on Internet). It was chaired by the former Spanish Prime Minister Felipe Gonzalez. In the course of its work it heard submissions from numerous eminent personalities and "think-tanks". In the end, its collective wisdom amounted to some thirty pages, mostly unoriginal and unexceptional, but it stressed that Europe is at a turning-point, faced by challenges which require joint action, in particular strengthening "economic governance", the "Single Market", etc.

[6] See http://esa.un.org/unpd/wpp2008/index.htm: UN *World Population Prospects*. I am surprised that these demographic projections – much more reliable than economic forecasts – get relatively little attention. "Net reproduction rates" – i.e. number of daughters per woman – in most Western European countries are around 0.8. This is to some extent offset by rising life expectancy; nevertheless, unless net immigration continues at approximately the present rate, total population will decline and the average age will rise.

In Russia, the net reproduction rate is even lower, though there seems to be some recent increase, and life expectancy (at birth) has been falling: it is only about 66 years overall and just 60 years for males. Consequently, with net migration assumed at some 50,000 per year, total population is projected fall from 140 million in 2010 to 116 million by 2050 (the UN medium assumption).

[7] These enlargement criteria were established by the Copenhagen European Council in 1993 and strengthened by the Madrid European Council in 1995.

[8] The European Neighbourhood Policy (ENP) was developed in 2004, with the objective of avoiding the emergence of new dividing lines between the enlarged EU and its neighbours and instead strengthening the prosperity, stability and security of all concerned. It offers:

"a privileged relationship, building upon a mutual commitment to common values (democracy and human rights, rule of law, good governance, market economy principles and sustainable development) ... The ENP remains distinct from the process of enlargement although it does not prejudice, for European neighbours, how their relationship with the EU may develop in future, in accordance with Treaty provisions."

The ENP applies to Armenia, Azerbaijan, Belarus, Georgia, Moldova and Ukraine; also to Algeria, Egypt, Israel, Jordan, Lebanon, Libya, Morocco, Occupied Palestinian Territory, Syria and Tunisia.

[9] It is probably an omission on my part that I have said nothing about the Council of Europe (based in Strasbourg) in these pages; the fact is that I know very little about it. Its website defines its objectives as follows:

> "to create a common democratic and legal area throughout the whole of the continent, ensuring respect for its fundamental values: human rights, democracy and the rule of law. These values are the foundations of a tolerant and civilised society and indispensable for European stability, economic growth and social cohesion. On the basis of these fundamental values, we try to find shared solutions to major problems such as terrorism, organised crime and corruption, cybercrime, bioethics and cloning, violence against children and women, and trafficking in human beings. Co-operation between all Member States is the only way to solve the major problems facing society today."

The Council of Europe has however no powers of enforcement.

[10] Cf. the UN *World Population Prospects* already cited.

[11] The "Reflection Group" accepted the need for more immigrants to offset the decline in the native EU population, but it did not consider the cultural conflicts liable to arise, particularly over Moslem immigration; and though it considered that the EU should fulfil its commitments to countries which have asked to accede to the EU, including Turkey, it failed to consider the political or economic implications.

[12] Christopher Caldwell, *Reflections on the Revolution in Europe – Can Europe be the same with different people in it?* (2009).

[13] The quotation on Russia is from an article by Sir Rodric Braithwaite in the *Financial Times* of 6 November 2009.

[14] This relative decline in scientific research in Russia is documented in *Web Science Database* from Thomson Reuters (January 2010), which writes:

> "The 1991 dissolution of the Soviet Union, not surprisingly, brought drastic political, economic and intellectual changes with which Russia has continued to grapple. Those forces have combined with particular effect on its research base. For one thing, budgets for science and technology have been sharply reduced. ... As a group, Russian scientists are aging—the average age for a member of the Russian Academy of Science is reportedly over 50. And, in opposition to the trend in growing research-based economies, their ranks are currently being depleted without sufficient replenishment by a new generation. In a 2006 Russian poll, only 1% of 1,600 respondents named science as a prestigious career, compared to work in the nation's petroleum

industry, or politics, or other fields. A serious 'brain drain' dates from the early 1990s, when, according to some estimates, upwards of 80,000 talented and able scientists left the country in search of better earnings, funding, and facilities abroad—to the benefit of Western Europe in particular."

[15] According to Human Rights Watch, since 2005 the European Court has held Russia responsible for the deaths of more than 200 people, mainly through killings and disappearances carried out by Russian forces in Chechnya. Two-thirds of the Chechnya judgments concern enforced disappearances, and the remaining ones, for the most part, extrajudicial killings, indiscriminate bombings, torture, and destruction of property. To date, Russia has not held a single individual accountable for the violations found in these rulings. At least 300 more cases concerning human rights violations in Chechnya and other republics in the North Caucasus are pending.

[16] This quotation is from an article by President Medvedev on the news web-site *Gazeta.ru*, quoted by the *Financial Times* of 13 October 2009.

[17] The report of the "Reflection Group" to the European Council, already mentioned, makes some useful general points on defence policy, but it has nothing to say about Russia or its neighbours. There is more substance in papers by the European Union Institute for Security Studies, based in Paris.

[18] The NATO-Russia Founding Act on Mutual Relations, Cooperation and Security was adopted in 1997, followed in 2002 by the establishment of the NATO-Russia Council. The NATO website says that in this framework, NATO member states and Russia work as equal partners in areas of common interest, and that cooperation is being intensified in a number of key areas: these include the fight against terrorism, crisis management, non-proliferation, arms control and confidence-building measures, missile defence, logistics, military cooperation, defence reform and civil emergencies.

[19] These national income statistics are World Bank data for 2008: http://web.worldbank.org – "Data and Statistics". GDP data are unreliable at best, and relationships will have changed due to the 2008/9 financial crisis, but the orders of magnitude remain valid.

Annex I
1989 – the opening of the frontiers

The twentieth anniversary of the fall of the Berlin Wall in 1989 led to a flurry of interest; facts that were not widely known appeared in TV and radio documentaries, notably by the Franco-German channel Arte and the BBC World Service, which have included eye-witness accounts. There are also numerous versions of these events on Internet.

More credit should be given to President Gorbachev than was realised at the time. Already in October 1985 he had told Warsaw Pace leaders that each ruling party must from then on take responsibility for its own affairs. In the Soviet Union itself, he had initiated political change which led to elections in March 1989 in which many old party hardliners were ousted.

In East Germany – the *Deutsche Demokratische Republik* – the authorities had already been much concerned in May 1989 by reports that the Hungarians were removing their frontier fence and had made representations to the Hungarian government, without success; they also asked Moscow to intervene, but Gorbachev said it was a matter for the Hungarians. The prospect of getting through the Hungarian-Austrian border caused an increased number of East Germans to go to Hungary for their summer holiday, especially to camp-sites on Lake Balaton.

The actual opening of the Hungarian-Austrian border on 19 August 1989 is a case of history apparently being made by one man, though something similar would no doubt have happened anyway. It probably suited the authorities in Budapest very well to leave the orders vague – they could disclaim responsibility if something went wrong. The officer in charge of the frontier post, Árpád Bella, was initially reprimanded for his inaction but later reprieved. To some Hungarians he remained a traitor, to others (the majority) a hero.

The resulting exodus of so many citizens added to unrest in the DDR. There were massive demonstrations in all the major cities, often severely repressed by the police. But in Leipzig on 9 October a huge crowd successfully braved the police, with the slogan "We are the people". Here too, brave actions by individuals played a key role. A cameraman from East Berlin (Hilbert Schefke) was allowed by the minister of the Nikolaikirche (Christian Führer) to film the events from the church tower; both were taking considerable risks. His film was smuggled into West Germany where it was shown on television, which East Germans could see, giving encouragement to further demonstrations.

On 18 October the party central committee removed its leader Erich Honecker and replaced him by Egon Krenz, but this failed to calm the people. On 9 November the committee agreed in principle to allow travel to the west. At the subsequent press conference their spokesman, Günther Schabowski – who had not been present at that meeting – read out the decision but did not notice that it was to come into effect only the following day. This information spread like wildfire and caused a great rush to the frontier posts; in the confusion, even the border guards did not know what to do, but the crowds became too great to contain.

The interpretation of these events has given rise to numerous works, one of the main questions being whether the communist regimes "imploded" either because of their own contradictions or as result of action by reformists within the system (Hungary, Poland?), or whether they were overthrown by popular revolt (Romania?). An excellent article in the *Times Literary Supplement* of 30 October 2009 reviews four recent works on the subject: Victor Sebestyen, *Revolution 1989*; Constantine Pleshakov, *There is No Freedom without Bread*; Michael Meyer, *The Year that changed the World*; Stephen Kotkin with Jan T. Gross, *Uncivil Society*.

Annex II
1989 – before and after

In October 2009 the BBC World Service broadcast a series of "cross-generational" dialogues, entitled "Children of the Revolution". Texts of the Russian, Polish, Romanian and East German interviews were made available on the BBC website. The recorded texts have been slightly edited and abbreviated.

RUSSIA

The speaker is Yevgeny Bely, 54, living in a province south-east of Moscow, a director of an Institute of Business and Economics, and he is talking with his son Mikhail.

Mikhail: So what did people hope for in those days? Were there any particular ideals?

Yevgeny: There were expectations. People hoped that the Soviet Communist Party would collapse, that there would no longer be any KGB. They hoped Party members would be banned from taking up managerial positions, that they would finally open up the borders and that people would be allowed to go abroad. The biggest hope people held was that they would get freedom –

freedom to speak, hear and read what they wanted. However, back then few people could really foresee what was to come.

Mikhail: So can you now say whether or not people have actually won anything as a result of the changes that happened? Have their hopes come to fruition?

Yevgeny: It might sound like a paradox, but it was the people associated with the Party who adapted best to the new way of life. If you look at today's bankers and businessmen, nearly all of them came from the *Komsomol* (Lenin's Communist Youth League).
And meanwhile those who came off worse were the scientists, academics and engineers who worked in the defence industry: they were simply left high and dry – some of them went off and worked on the markets, others worked assembling furniture. Ideological people lost out, such as the history teachers and political scientists...
I actually believe that the people who lost out the most were those who went on the rallies; that section of the population who listened to (iconic Soviet singer-songwriter Vladimir) Vysotsky, who read Pasternak in secret, who listened to Voice of America radio. It was the beginning of tough and anarchistic market relations. Only bandits - and people who could protect themselves from those bandits – survived.

Mikhail: And did it get better or worse?

Yevgeny: That's difficult to answer. Consider the situation: in 1989 I was 34 years old and had a PhD. It automatically meant a 500-rouble salary – the same as a chief engineer or general would have been receiving. Your grandfather, who was also a professor, could go on holiday to the spa town of Kislovodsk. He had a good car and a *dacha*. By those times, he was a pretty well-off and highly respected person. Nowadays someone with a PhD who works at a university all too often lives considerably worse off than the owner of some run-down tobacconist's. The obvious pluses from the changes have been the consumer possibilities – like, going on holiday abroad, buying all sorts of goods that we'd never seen before.

Mikhail: But many people now complain that the role of social protection has greatly reduced.

Yevgeny: That's true. I wasn't afraid, then, that I would live in poverty, once I became a pensioner. Now that's a very real fear.

Mikhail: Where there any side effects to the emergence of those freedoms?

Yevgeny: I'm convinced that back then people were a damn sight more intellectual: people used to read – artistic novels, big thick magazines. Society was more educated, less wishy-washy. I never knew the country could change so much in the space of twenty years; that people like doctors and teachers would start thieving, taking bribes, giving people low grades so people would pay for extra lessons. The idea that two decades on the country could have deteriorated so far morally - never even entered my head. That's what has really shocked me.

ROMANIA

During the unrest preceding the fall of the communist regime in December 1989, Ioan Savu openly confronted the authorities, shouting that the protest leaders are ready to die for their freedom. His son Adrian was eleven years' old at the time. He now works for the European Union and is a father of three children.

Adrian: How do you remember 1989, and the meaning of those events?

Ioan: For me, 1989 was the purest moment of my life. It was the first time I felt truly relieved. That unique state of mind, that feeling of freedom, has always existed and is still there in our hometown of Timisoara.
Before taking to the streets I had a long discussion with your mother. I convinced her that I could not keep on living with that 'rat mentality' anymore. Something needed to be done. I told her "what if something happens and I am not there? How will I look my children in the eye?"
The risks were huge for all of us, but someone had to start the change. We can't always wait for the other person to make the first step.

Adrian: At the time, I didn't realise the risks you were taking. They just told us to prepare to leave home. I was eleven and could not understand the danger we were exposed to. I just remember you shaving off your beard – a clear sign that we were going into hiding. In fact it was quite exciting; hiding was something we did a lot during the communist era. I later realised the magnitude of this decision and now, as a parent myself, I know there is no sacrifice you wouldn't do for your own children.

Ioan: Your words bring up memories from my own childhood. I was a kid, no older than you were in 1989. My father refused to join the communist agricultural collective, so they took everything from us. The cows, the bricks we saved to build a new home, our clothes. Everything. When there was nothing left they pointed a gun to my father's chest and asked him to sign the papers, to agree to join them. He said "shoot me, I will still not do it!"
In the 1950s, when whole families simply disappeared overnight, my mother fell ill. Her heart just couldn't cope with the tension. She never fully recovered from that. That's why I have never been able to live with the idea of communism. There was no room for it in my heart or my mind.

Adrian: Something I disagreed with you after 1989 was your decision not to get involved in politics. I believe it was difficult to take this kind of responsibility, with so many former communist figures keeping their prominent positions even after the regime fell. But now our society is struggling with people and mentalities of the past.

Ioan: At the time, we all knew very well what we didn't want anymore. But we didn't know what we wanted or how to achieve what we wanted. We assumed everything would change by itself. We were simply naïve, and I was one of the naïve ones, I admit that. Before 1989 I had made a number of attempts to leave the country, which always ended in failure. If things hadn't changed in 1989, I would have eventually left.

Adrian: We would have survived in communist times, but for us it's definitely much better now. However the country still has serious social problems. Before 1989, communism was like a giant umbrella covering all citizens. Everyone was under that umbrella whether they wanted it or not. The individuals had become completely dependent of the system. The system made them unresponsive, unable to take initiatives. That has been quite obvious since 1989. Whenever we had social problems, or even natural disasters, we just didn't react.

POLAND

In 1989 Maciek Reszczynski had already left Poland and was working for the BBC in London. But in 1990 he took his daughter Niamh back to see the country for the first time. They now have Irish nationality.

Maciek: In August 1990 I was a young journalist - I'd just started working for the BBC and I spent my first year reporting on the Berlin Wall. For me Berlin was such a symbol. When I was younger, we'd travel from Poland to East Berlin and we'd go to the television tower. Everybody was on the western side and it looked like the television tower was going to topple over because it was so overloaded with people. Then in August 1990 I just packed you and your sister in the car and we went to Poland through East Germany. We had a holiday and on the way back there was no East Germany anymore! The country disappeared while we were holidaying. So on the way back, we took a break in Berlin.

Niamh: I don't remember a huge amount about it. Klara and I were four and five years old at the time. Do you remember having to explain to us why the Berlin Wall and its fall were important?

Maciek: You were both born not long after the end of martial law in Poland. I don't know if you remember, but while other children learned nursery rhymes you were taught to chant 'Lech Walesa, Lech Walesa'. So you had a clue about Solidarnosc and Walesa, and the Berlin wall falling was part of all that.

Niamh: At such a young age I don't really remember understanding what Solidarity meant.

Maciek: When you were at that young age it was important for me to show it to you while it was still there. It delineated a very firm boundary in my life growing up, because I couldn't travel. In fact, I remember as a teenager I dreamt about going abroad, and about going to the West.

Niamh: Was the physical nature of the journey - especially driving through Germany - symbolic of the difficulty of crossing borders and travelling that you had experienced?

Maciek: Yes, absolutely. I crossed the border a couple of times when East Germany was still in business. In a way I kind of miss it. At the time, I could hardly imagine anything more exciting than going from West Berlin to East Berlin and back. Everything would change completely. You went from little Trabant cars to big shiny cars, and from half empty shops to shops full of goods. And people were relaxed and it was different – a different planet just a stone's throw away.

Niamh: I can imagine it being a good educational tool. As a child, you have a certain innocence and naivety when you think of communism because it seems like such a great idea. Travelling back and forth must have been quite a good physical example of the experience that you had of communism.

Maciek: Well you know people talk a lot of rubbish about communism. I liked communism because I had lots of girlfriends! But overall, yes, it was a dreadful system. I must say that last year, in 2008, we drove to Poland and nobody was interested in looking at our passports. For me it's a big deal because I grew up in a completely divided Europe, and that's what I wanted you and Klara to see, which is why I took you back in 1990.

Niamh: There's a picture of Klara and me holding bits of the Berlin Wall.

Maciek: Well, that's what we went to see, we went to see it with our own eyes. I think that happens at those moments, you feel the wind of history.

Niamh: Those memories feel very significant to me. It's really hard for me to wrap my head around the fact that communism and martial-law happened in Europe, in our lifetime. In the internet age that we live in, I can't imagine a situation in which communication can be cut off between countries. I won't even bother asking whether something like that could happen now because I don't believe that it can.

Maciek: If it wasn't for Solidarity, for martial law and for what martial law was a result of, you wouldn't be here. There were very few people travelling between Ireland and Poland (which is unthinkable today with hundreds of Poles in Ireland) but your mum and I started something really new and unusual in those days. So in a way Klara and you coming into the world marked the beginning of the end of one era, and the fact that you guys can travel freely whether you have Polish passports or Irish passports. Now Ryanair flies to Wroclaw, my home town: this would have felt like science fiction when I was growing up, when I was your age!

Niamh: Polish martial law ended in 1983, but its hold was prevalent throughout the 1980s. How was the news of the breakdown of communism relayed to you through radio, television, and through being at the BBC?

Maciek: The Solidarity revolution in Poland was a photocopy revolution. There's a healthy little theory that without the photocopier - which was a way of breaking the state's monopoly on printing - it would have been very difficult.
But that was 1980. 1989 was distinctively a fax revolution. Being a journalist here in Bush House in 1989, most of the stuff we got through the Iron Curtain was via fax. Poland's only free daily paper, which was set up to report the first democratic elections, would be photocopied in Warsaw and faxed to us. This was all pre-internet. It is very difficult to conceive today that news travelled like that. And suddenly the Berlin Wall fell in the autumn of 1989, and by spring 1990, Polish BBC programmes were broadcast on FM by Polish state radio.

Niamh: So your family would have had access to news.

Maciek: Yes, they could see our faces. This was a new era. Only a few years previously a Bulgarian journalist who worked in Bush House was killed by communist intelligence for being a "traitor", so there was a lot of fear. When I came to the Polish section a lot of people appeared on air with adopted surnames, you know very strange sounding names. And then after the wall fell, many of them reverted back to their real names.

Niamh: Lech Walesa was elected president in October 1990. Did you vote? Could you vote?

Maciek: I did better than that, I went to see him. I got the best gig of my journalistic career. To top all these great things that happened, there was a matter of the 1936 Polish constitution, which established the idea of the continuity of Polish statehood. All the while during communism, there was in fact a Polish president-in-exile, Ryszard Kaczorowski, living in London, who had in his possession the great seal of state. From the point of view of the pre-war constitution the Polish communist government was not legitimate.
So when Walesa was elected, Kaczorowski took the seal of office, the constitution and all the other symbols of the Polish Republic and flew to Warsaw to hand them over, to emphasise the continuity of free Poland. And I got on the plane which carried this guy to Poland with the seal. And I got to talk to Kaczorowski, the president-in-exile. I had my microphone in his face, I was asking 'so how are you feeling?' and he was saying 'well I haven't been to Poland since 1939 so this is going to be really emotional for me.'
And then, as I'm recording, the captain says in Polish 'ladies and gentlemen, we have crossed the Polish border and we are now flying over the territory of Poland' and this guy started crying into the microphone, literally his tears

were dropping onto the microphone and he's saying 'see the pilot just said...' this is what was happening. So it was quite momentous, 1989.

EAST GERMANY

Karin, a 51-year-old teacher who lived, studied and worked in the former German Democratic Republic, talks to her daughter Katrin, a 28-year old social education worker. Today they both live in Bremerhaven in the Federal Republic of Germany.

Katrin: So what happened when you applied to leave the GDR? What did the government do to you?

Karin: When I applied for an exit visa I lost my job as a teacher. I couldn't work anymore and didn't receive any financial support. It was horrible.

Katrin: So what were your expectations of West Germany, before you left?

Karin: At that time I had no idea what it would be like in the West. My attitude towards West Germany was actually quite negative. If my husband wasn't living over there, I would never have applied for an exit visa from the GDR on my own. But I was pleasantly surprised. Everybody really cared about me and were nice to me. The social services department paid me an unemployment compensation. I received an interest-free loan and after six months I got a job.

Katrin: So looking back, was it the right choice for you to leave the GDR?
Karin: Definitely yes. There was no real perspective in the GDR, no possibility of doing something else. Career choices were controlled and you could not even choose academic subjects on your own. Life was secure, but also really tight.

Katrin: In what way?

Karin: Concerning daily needs. It was quite cheap, but clothes, shoes and cars were really expensive and we lived in a horrible satellite town, made with precast concrete slabs. We never had the opportunity in the GDR, as we did in the West, to go on a school exchange to England or France. Even to Russia,' where nobody wanted to go, it was really difficult to go there...

Katrin: But you seem to be quite happy about how things worked out for you personally after the fall of the Berlin Wall.

Karin: Yes, it all worked out for the best and I definitely don't want to have the GDR back. For probably about ten years I had dreams during the night that I had to return to the GDR and live there. But luckily that was just a nightmare.

Index of persons and places

also by Michael Tracy:

THE WORLD OF THE EDWARDIAN CHILD

as seen in Arthur Mee's "Children's Encyclopædia", 1908–1910

Based on articles in the first edition of the famous *Children's Encyclopædia*, edited by Arthur Mee, this book provides vivid insights into how people lived in the Edwardian era, what they thought and how they brought up their children.

Michael Tracy has distilled over five thousand pages into a couple of hundred, making extensive use of original illustrations.

The book asks how the upbringing of that generation prepared them for the Great War of 1914–18 and its aftermath, and whether the Edwardian confidence in Britain's enduring power has continued to hamper Britain's adjustment to loss of Empire and a reduced role in the world.

For more information
and to order,
go to www.HermitageBook.net

Lightning Source UK Ltd.
Milton Keynes UK
06 December 2010